MADNESS
MIRACLES
MILLIONS

MADNESS
MIRACLES
MILLIONS

"Be inspired, encouraged, and motivated.
I was." —DEBBIE MACOMBER
#1 New York Times Best Selling Author

JOSEPH SEMPREVIVO
AND LARRY SEMPREVIVO

TATE PUBLISHING
AND ENTERPRISES, LLC

Published by Tate Publishing & Enterprises, LLC
127 E. Trade Center Terrace | Mustang, Oklahoma 73064 USA
1.888.361.9473 | www.tatepublishing.com

Tate Publishing is committed to excellence in the publishing industry. The company reflects the philosophy established by the founders, based on Psalm 68:11,
"The Lord gave the word and great was the company of those who published it."

Published in the United States of America

ISBN: 978-1-62295-881-8
1. Memoir
2. Business/Family
13.07.25

Contents

DEDICATION

Lawrence Semprevivo:
I dedicate this book to Josephine Marie (Jo Marie) and my three children; Palma, Lawrence Jr. and Joseph.

Joseph Semprevivo:
Dedicated to my mom, dad, wife and four little ones: Joseph II, Giorgio, Giovanni, Palma.

Betty and Al Gasperi:
For your unconditional love, not only during the accident, but throughout our lives.

Adrian Gonzales:
For giving up your days and nights off to deliver cookies, do demos and work in the factory with me.

ACKNOWLEDGMENTS

To my mom and dad whose love, support, and dedication to family values has helped guide me throughout my life. Our conversations each morning and evening keep me focused and driven in life.

To my best friend and lovely wife, Memory, whose unselfish love, support, and loyalty never goes unnoticed. Thanks for always understanding the late nights and long work-filled weeks.

To Palma, my wonderful sister, who has always offered unlimited support and love, and who knows how to keep me laughing.

To Larry Jr, who sacrificed for years to help us get back on our feet.

To Rhett Palmer, who never stopped driving us to tell our story. Your support and excitement for this project is very important to me.

To Cassandra Woody whose thoughts, comments, and hard work made the book much better.

To Debbie Macomber, for taking the time to read the pages and giving amazing feedback.

To Anson Williams, for the never-ending positive support, insight, and spirit.

To Alex Cobb, for helping this book become a homerun.

To Chad Connelly, for the late night conversations about the manuscript, always pushing me to achieve more.

To Tony Defranco, for always believing in me and being there all of the time. You're a great friend.

To Tommy Giles, for amazing dedication and follow up. Very Impressive.

To Joe Ianelli, for being there when times were not only good, but also bad. I will never forget how you stood by our side during the accident.

To Del Rey Sena for the perfect brainstorming sessions that turned out excellent improvements.

CHAPTER ONE

THE ACCIDENT

W ith one hand reaching for the emergency stop button and the other being fed between two massive rollers that were slowly crushing everything they passed, Larry Semprevivo began to feel he was not going to be able to keep his cool for much longer. This didn't make any sense to him yet, the accident that is.

He was an experienced pressman and he was good at what he did. People with twenty years of experience under their belts did not get caught in these kinds of situations. He had done everything right that morning; everything he was trained to do. Before he started work, he put the machine on safety to be sure something like this would not happen. So why was it that he was staring death right in the face and listening to his own screams echo throughout the factory?

The reason Larry found himself in such a predicament that morning was this; someone had accidently taken the machine off safety while Larry was working to adjust the plates in the cylinders of the two story high printing press that he knew very well at that point in his life. Experience and caution can get you a long way in a factory, but it can't save you when someone else makes a mistake. Larry was learning that lesson on the fly right now.

While the rollers worked their way from his fingers to his hand, crushing everything as they went, Larry could only watch helplessly as his arm bubbled on his side of the rollers. Muscle, tendons, bones, and blood were all being squeezed from his fingers up to his hand, then to his wrist and finally into his arm. Larry sat, swallowing back the fear and panic that was swelling up, making its way into the back of his throat from the pit of his stomach, and stared down at his arm that was now bulging. Sweat beaded up over his entire body and dampened his work clothes. His eyes seemed to widen in proportion to the swelling of his arm.

"Stop the damn press!" Larry yelled as he watched his arm disappear behind rollers that were intended to put varnish on baseball cards. On a normal day, Larry watched as the printing press pumped out full sheets of baseball cards, bringing the images and stats of Thurman Munson, Steve Garvey, and Dusty Baker to the world. This day would not be a normal day. This day would be the mark of a new phase in Larry's life, but he would have to make it through it first.

As Larry was being sucked through the press feeder, he could not figure out why no one was stopping the machine. His initial call for help had worked contrary to its intentions and, after the last syllable left his mouth, the entire plant froze with fear and then erupted into chaos. No one could tell where the shout was coming from, so it seemed that everyone just assumed that someone else was rushing to aid whoever it was in danger. This phenomenon in which everyone assumes that someone else will help in an emergency situation is actually so common that it has a name, two actually; this is called bystander effect or Genovese syndrome. That day, Genovese Syndrome was threatening Larry's life.

From the moment the press was turned on and feeding his arm through an apparatus intended to glaze baseball cards, Larry had begun reaching for the emergency shut off button. After his first call for help went unanswered, Larry strained even harder to touch the magical little button that was his only prayer. He reached out to hit the button, but it was just out of reach. The tips of his right fingers were inches, if that, from the button. Larry realized right at that moment that life and death could be measured in seconds and centimeters.

Larry's fingers stretched for that button that had become so significant and they burned and tingled with want. His skin went hot and then turned ice cold as his brain tried to catch up with what was going on. He knew that he had to stay calm, but his heart slammed against his rib cage and he had to work hard not to let his mind fall into panic mode.

There is nothing so terrifying as watching powerlessly as your chances of survival tick away with the turning of cogs in a machine that has you trapped. This had to be what it felt like to drown. Flailing out in the ocean able to see the shore but being swept out by the tide with every new wave.

Larry had always been known for his levelheadedness and ability to solve any problem that life could throw at him, no matter how difficult. It was devastating to lose that ability so abruptly.

He had no control over the machine now and he knew that. Resolve to keep his cool was all that Larry had at this point and he clung to it; no machine or mishap would ever rob him of it.

Still struggling to get to the emergency shut off switch and using every ounce of energy to keep himself calm, Larry became very aware of everything around him. Time felt like it had slowed down and his senses seemed to sharpen. Everything around him came into focus, but was suddenly drowned out by a thunderous hum that filled every square inch of the factory.

"Stop the damn press!" Larry yelled again as his arm was being consumed.

All the sights, sounds, and scents that surrounded him were eclipsed by the overwhelming resonance of that mysterious hum. He was shaken by that strange sound that had now encompassed his entire being. Larry had no idea what the hum was or where it came from, but he let it drown out the chaos of the factory while he took deep breaths and watched the rollers devour more of his arm.

The chemical smell of grease and varnish began to turn his stomach, as he was pulled further into the machine. Why was no one turning off the press? He stared down at his own arm, now looking as if it were on the verge of bursting, filled with sinew and blood. His skin wouldn't be able to handle this much longer and the ability to hit the emergency shut off had vanished behind the other side of the rollers along with his left forearm.

Finally, unable to think of anything else to do, Larry let out another scream. The scream merged with the resounding hum and a chill went down the backs of everyone in the plant. At the moment that his voice faded and the last bit of breath was let out into the air around him, the machine stopped. Larry was shocked. It had really stopped, and so had the disappearance of his left arm. He knew that it lay crushed on the other side of the rollers, but he would not lose any more of his arm.

With the machine no longer feeding his appendages into two giant rollers, Larry assumed the hard part was over. With the press now off, a quiet settled over the factory for a split second, then a new level of chaos filled the entire factory. The building was like a beehive that had been hit with a baseball bat.

Soon, there arose from the swarm of disoriented workers two maintenance men to help Larry get out of the press. The men began disassembling the machine around him, taking off one piece after another as quickly as they could to free his crushed arm from the teeth of the metallic beast.

Larry breathed deeply and tried to remain absorbed in his breathing to distract himself from the smashed arm that laid waiting for him on the other side of the rollers.

Although his arm had been completely crushed, he had not felt anything yet because he had been so devoted to surviving. As the men pulled his arm out, however, a burning sensation started at his fingertips and worked its way up his arm, becoming more intense as it moved. It felt as if someone had doused his flesh in gasoline and set fire to it. Between the crushing and the chemical burn of the varnish, someone may as well have.

Once it was freed from the feeders, Larry's arm hung like dead weight against his left side. He knew that he needed to get to a hospital quick if he was going to have a chance at using the hardly recognizable limb, which now had the permanent markings of his favorite watch embedded into it.

Larry immediately stepped away from the machine, half dazed and still trying to grasp what had happened. The second he moved away the machine kicked back on. The entire factory hit a new level of pandemonium as each worker realized the machine had not been shut off; it had just suddenly stopped when Larry cried out. The machine stopped long enough for workers to remove Larry's damaged arm, but came on the moment he was out. No one could wrap their heads around how or why this happened. There was absolutely no explanation for it.

Larry stood and stared at the press, stunned as he watched all the parts around him come back to life. At that moment, the gravity of what had happened had not completely hit him. Everything that had occurred that day seemed to have taken place by happenstance, in both good and bad ways. Although he couldn't see the entire picture that at that moment and had no idea how meaningful the chain of events that happened that day were, he did grasp that something incredible had just occurred. That day he knew that there were more than printers and foremen in that printing press factory.

⟡

CHAPTER TWO

FINDING MIRACLES
IN MADNESS

U nfortunately, the chain of seemingly unfortunate
events did not stop as soon as Larry was freed
from the press. He was then placed on an old factory
gurney that ripped beneath his weight and sent him
tumbling to the concrete floor. Appreciating the
gesture, but concerned for his own safety, Larry decided
he would walk himself to the car that was waiting to
take him to the hospital.

Seeing the hospital in the distance, the frazzled
pressman finally let out a deep sigh that had been
trapped in his chest since the moment his arm was first
pulled into the rollers. Larry's well-being was about to
be placed into the hands of someone who could ensure
that everything would be fine.

The car pulled into the emergency entrance and
Larry, along with a couple of guys from the factory,
walked along the frozen sidewalk up to the dingy brick
building that stood before them. Passing through the
automatic doors, Larry made his way to the check in

desk and was immediately told that the hospital did not have the means to treat his kind of injury. Responsibility was handed right back to him.

He sucked the sigh of relief back into his lungs, and he held it there the entire drive to the second, larger hospital.

This time, Larry was admitted and doctors with white coats and stethoscopes began to treat his arm immediately, which was an immense comfort. As the nurses and doctors began to cut the shirt from Larry's mangled arm, they began to ask him questions.

"Can you feel the arm?" one doctor asked, inspecting the damage.

"It burns. It feels like it's on fire," Larry replied, looking at the doctor's face as he spoke.

"Are you allergic to anything?" the doctor followed, as his eyes remained fixed on the arm.

"Demerol," Larry answered quickly. He was now in the able hands of doctors and nurses. His heart rate finally began to slow and some of the tension left his muscles. He could also see that his wife, Josephine, and some of the guys from the factory had arrived. It seemed the nightmare was coming to an end.

As Larry began to relax a bit and let the doctors tend to his crushed arm, he suddenly broke out into a sweat. Within a matter of sixty seconds, his body was almost drenched. Something had gone terribly wrong.

"Did someone give me Demerol?" Larry asked, feeling the panic in his chest rise yet again. "Something is going on. Did I get Demerol?"

"Yes," a nurse responded, "we had to."

There was an obvious shift in the atmosphere at this point. The doctors asked everyone to leave the hospital; they said they needed to get Larry to a room. There was a new sense of urgency that settled on the medical staff, but it didn't seem to have anything to do with Larry's injured arm. It was obvious that something strange was going on. Josephine sat looking at the doctors a little perplexed.

"I'm sorry, Mr. and Mrs. Semprevivo. We can't do anything for you," the nurse was saying as she wheeled Larry down a long narrow hall whose florescent lights made everything look dingy and unwelcoming.

"What do you mean you can't do anything for us?" Josephine replied. "Where are we going?"

Larry laid completely still in the gurney as the nurse pushed him across the scuffed linoleum floors. Soaked with his own perspiration, his left shirtsleeve torn away, and his shattered arm resting at his side, Larry began to feel the same panic creeping in that had been picking at him while he was being eaten alive.

"I'm sorry, that is all we could do," the nurse said as she walked past the automatic hospital doors and pushed Larry into the snow filled parking lot. She handed Josephine an IV bag that had a hose trailing into Larry's arm, then turned and walked away. Right then both Larry and Josephine realized that the plan was never to move Larry to another room; it was to get him out of the hospital without a scene.

Josephine instantly scanned the parking lot for a payphone. She saw one 200 feet away and pushed the gurney through the snow covered sidewalks while holding the IV bag. She picked up the frozen receiver and called the only person she could think of, the family pediatrician, Dr. Grossman. Stunned by what he heard, the pediatrician told them to get to the hospital in Cherry Hill immediately and they would take care of him.

In the meantime, Bill Hadley, the feeder operator in training who had caused the accident, made his way to the hospital to check on Larry and apologize for what had happened. Larry spotted Bill and told Josephine to get his attention. They were going to need him to help get them to the Cherry Hill hospital as quickly as possible. How ironic that he would be a curse and a blessing in the same day.

Bill ran over to the stranded couple and the two explained what had happened. They told him they were in desperate need of his help. Bill was willing to do anything at that point to try to make up for what had happened, so he helped Larry into the car and began to make his way from Philadelphia to Cherry Hill, New Jersey.

As they crossed the Ben Franklin Bridge, the car was completely silent. As Larry sat and examined his own arm that lay lifeless in his lap, blue and crippled, he quietly prayed. He prayed to God for help. He knew that this was a crisis situation, so he stayed quiet and prayed. Making their way over that bridge, Bill drove, Josephine silently wept, and Larry prayed.

True to his word, the pediatrician was waiting with help. Larry was admitted once again, but this time he was not kicked out. The arm was cleaned and casted, but circulation was still not making it to his fingers. The doctors discussed amputation, but Larry would not hear of it. He prayed even harder and God must have been listening.

As he sat in his hospital room one day, an intern passed by and saw his arm. He came in and looked over it, asking Larry what had happened. As Larry explained his injury, the intern seemed to light up, which was a strange reaction to such a story.

The reason the intern was so excited about Larry's tragedy was that he had been studying injuries just like Larry's. He wanted to treat the arm himself. *Quite a strange turn of events*, Larry thought to himself.

It occurred to him as the intern began to explain his interest in Larry's situation that we are not put through obstacles to suffer; we are brought through obstacles to see something better on the other side.

The intern cut the cast off and began to administer blood thinner to get the circulation to Larry's fingers. Although Larry still didn't have use of his fingers, amputation was no longer a consideration. A full recovery was the goal now. Larry felt a calm settle over him and knew that this intern wasn't a coincidence; he was an answer to a prayer. The next day, God made sure that Larry would know He was with him. The Monsignor came in and prayed with Larry. He blessed him with this; "From the power of prayer of children, you will be fine."

From that point on, Larry knew that things were going to change for him and his family. Something had happened that day his arm was pulled into the printing press, and it was bigger than an arm injury or the obstacle he faced trying to find help after the accident. Larry would learn how mysterious God really was, and also learn never to look at a situation the same way again.

On the day that overwhelming hum filled the factory while Larry was face to face with death, he learned that we have a lot more control over our lives than we realize; not in the things that happen though, but in how we handle them. The lessons learned from the accident would shape the Semprevivo family for the rest of their lives. Each child would experience first-hand what a life filled with a positive attitude and mutual gratitude could create. One of those children was me, Joseph Semprevivo. Larry and Josephine Semprevivo are my parents, and, although I was not born when the accident happened, the values my father always had combined with the lesson he learned from that tragedy would go on to mold me into who I am today.

You see, I have managed to create a company that I am pretty proud of, both for its success and because of everything it stands for. I wouldn't have been able to do it without my family. There was a very unique process that brought my company into being and allowed it to blossom into what it is today, and the process began with my dad's accident.

To appreciate the success I have had, it's vital to know where I came from. My success lies in my past. Don't worry about the vagueness of the company just yet. You'll get it all by the end. The focal point of my success isn't really in what I have built today, after all; the focal point is the path I took to get there.

Every success has a genesis; some are rooted in luck, while others may come about from the very opposite. It sounds strange I know, that success would come to those who are void of luck. That is really how it happened, though. You see, my family has been very unlucky in some ways, but absolutely blessed in others. What we have found during our many trials is this: life isn't about luck, it's about attitude. Luck you have no control over, but attitude is something that you always have a choice about. How you interpret and handle the situations you come across will dictate your life. You need proof? I've got just that for you. We'll have to jump back to my mom and dad.

CHAPTER THREE

SECOND CHANCES

A fter the accident, my dad felt very blessed in many ways. For every terrible event that happened that day, a miracle followed close behind. That would be the theme of our lives from that point on. Our blessings were always the rainbow after a terrible storm. Instead of feeling downtrodden by the fact that it often took hardship to find happiness, we have all developed an attitude of hopefulness during times of adversity. A perfect example of that is my existence. I'll explain what I mean by that.

I left off with my dad in the hands of an intern who specialized in his exact type of injury. The intern had done everything he could to help my dad's arm heal and to prevent amputation, but after two days, he could still not feel or move his fingers, which meant circulation had not returned to them. The intern that was treating my dad met with other doctors to discuss possible solutions. They collectively decided to try putting leeches on the tips of his fingers. This suggestion seemed a little archaic, and my dad couldn't help but think of George Washington's fatal leech experience, so he was not looking forward to the antiquated approach to medicine. Thankfully, the very next day, my dad regained feeling and movement. The intern could leave the leeches in their containers and my dad could finally look forward to going home. Thanksgiving was rapidly approaching and he wasn't about to spend it in the hospital.

Finally, on Thanksgiving Day, my dad was given a clean bill of health (or at least a cleaned up bill of health) and sent on his way. Unfortunately, Murphy's Law doesn't take holidays. On the way out, my dad was walking down the hospital deck and fell, slamming down onto his back. My mom, of course, was mortified and rushed to help. After all he had gone through, this was the last thing he needed.

"Larry! Oh my gosh, Larry!" my mom gasped as she ran to my dad, dropping the bags and her purse that she had been carrying.

"Let me call an orderly, Larry. Are you okay? I'm so sorry, honey. This is just awful," my mom was saying as she put her arms around my dad and held him close to her.

My dad looked up at my mom as she scrambled to help him to his feet and he saw something that he had never noticed in her before. He saw her strength. Sure, he had always known my mom was amazing, that's why he married her, but he saw in her something that he didn't know she had.

When everything seemed to begin to crumble around them, my mother was able to put the pieces back together and make everything whole again. He saw that this woman would always make sure her family was okay, no matter what it took. He had always assumed up to that point that he was the one that did that, but it was her all along. She was just amazing enough to let him think that he was the strong one. A new kind of love swelled in my dad's heart that day as he took my mom's hand while he laid there on the cold, damp cement.

"No, honey, I'm fine. We're going home today. I am going home with my wife today and I am going to hug my kids," was my dad's response, as he got back on his feet and helped my mom pick up the bags she dropped.

The entire ride home, the car was quiet, just as it had been on the ride over the Ben Franklin Bridge from Philadelphia to New Jersey the day of my dad's accident. This was a different quiet, though; it was a reverent quiet. My dad sat and looked at my mom as she drove them home and he thanked God that He had given him such a woman. He thanked God for everything, for being with him through the accident, for the intern who had helped them, and for the beautiful children he was on his way home to be with.

Lost in thought and happy to be sitting next to his soul mate, Larry realized that this second chance meant a lot. He didn't want to miss out on why God had saved him, so he would keep his eyes open and his outlook positive from that point forward.

As they drove home that cold November day, he also decided that the Semprevivos were lacking something; they needed something more to complete them. That more he was thinking of was me. Instead of obsessing over how life would be post-accident or fretting over what they would do next, my parents decided that they were ready for another tiny body to love.

My dad says that something happened the day of the accident and that something inside him was stirred. He had the strongest desire to have another child. There was a new love that consumed him, and he wanted another child to pass that love to. They got that tiny body a year later on November 1, 1971.

Although my parents were optimistic and seemed to only grow closer after the accident, people outside of our direct family didn't possess the same attitude. My dad went to work on a winter morning Larry Semprevivo, but had returned home from the hospital a stranger to many of our friends and even family members. My parents had no idea what it was about the accident that caused loved ones to vanish, whether it was the fear of my family asking for help or the awkwardness of not knowing what to say in the wake of the accident. Regardless of the reason behind their absence, the desertion that my family experienced in a time of need made a bigger impact than the accident had. My dad will tell you that the scars left by the abandonment of loved ones were much deeper than the scars left on his arm by the printing press.

The months following the printing press ordeal would truly try my parents' faith and patience. Within only a few days of being home, it was clear that this next phase of their life would have far fewer people in it. With the exception of my mother's Aunt Betty, my dad's brother Joseph, and my dad's best friend, Joe Iannelli, my family was on its own. This was painful, but it was nothing that my parents couldn't overcome and they both knew that. So, instead of fixating on their losses, my mom and dad decided to put their energy and faith in those who they knew they could count on. In the wake of the accident my family became closer than ever.

It was at that point right after the accident when so many "friends" disappeared that my parents began to truly realize that life was what you made of it and that bad things were bound to happen to everyone. What separated the victors from the defeated was what you did with your life in the wake of tragedy. Some people make excuses and some people make a new life. My parents decided to make a new life and to build it on the foundation of the genuine friends and dedicated family that stuck by their sides. In the end, my parents saw that the accident really didn't rob my family of friendships; it purged them of people who weren't worthy of being in their lives and gave them a stronger and more reliable foundation to stand on—a smaller foundation, maybe, but it's quality, not quantity in all aspects of life.

⸺⁐⁑⁐⸺

CHAPTER FOUR

REBUILDING

My dad went without work for some time because with only one good arm and twenty years of experience as a pressman, your options for work are limited. As time passed, finances became tighter and tighter and the situation began to look pretty grim.

Paychecks stopped coming, but the bills did not. It wasn't long until the mortgage was due, but there was nothing to pay it with. My dad went to the Union to see if anything could be done. The entire situation was a little confounding, as he had been injured on the job by no fault of his own, but was in no way being taken care of now. Surely the Union, an organization created to represent the working class, would do something.

When my dad finished speaking with the Union representatives, he was left with two options; he could either drop his pension and take home $2,500.00, or he could leave his pension alone and let his family starve and his house go into foreclosure. My dad knew that giving up his pension was no small thing, but his family needed food to eat and a home to eat it in, so he took his $2,500.00 and went home. So much for Union dues.

For a family of four that is working on a fifth, $2,500.00 only lasts so long. Along with struggling to pay bills, my dad's arm was still in bad shape and he needed a lot of physical therapy, but after sixty days without work, the Union cut off my dad's insurance. Because of the bureaucracy involved, it would also be months before worker's compensation would step in to do anything. Being caught between a sixty day insurance cut off and a six month wait for worker's comp was a true revelation for my father that there is no safety net for the middleclass.

While my dad worked to figure out how to keep the family afloat, my mom had gone out and purchased a small printing press from a family friend. My mom figured that if no one would hire my dad with his injury, she would bring the work home and she would learn to be a provider as well.

My mom and dad set the printing press up in our garage and my dad taught my mom how everything worked. It took her hardly any time at all to get the hang of the contraption and in no time my parents were printing flyers for a local drug store. My mom worked nonstop between taking care of the kids and printing fliers, and she never once complained or acted as if she were bitter about the situation. She knew that my dad's heart was broken by everything that had happened between the loss of friends and the slow progress of regaining use of his arm. She didn't care that my dad wasn't able to work at that time; all she cared about was maintaining a secure and loving home for her family, and that she did.

Night after night she proved the love and dedication she had to her family as she spent hours hunched over a small printing press pumping out fliers that displayed the weekly specials on laundry detergent, hand soap, and baby food. Again, my dad saw the strength in her he had seen the day he fell outside the hospital. She was more than a wife and mother and he knew that now; this woman was his own angel.

While my parents' independent printing business slowly grew in the garage, my dad slowly realized that something more than physical therapy would have to be done if he wanted to use his arm again. After a very long six months, his workers' comp finally went into effect and he was able to see a doctor who thought he could help.

The circumstances in which the doctor could help were a bit strange. He was a German doctor and he wanted to do a surgery to try to repair my dad's arm. That part of it may not seem so extraordinary; the catch was that the surgery had never been done before and my dad would have to remain lucid during the entire procedure so the doctors would know if he could use his fingers. Not only would he be the first person to undergo the surgery, the entire process was going to be recorded to use for other doctors to help treat patients in the future.

The surgery seemed like a long shot, but my dad was still not able to use his hand, so he was willing to invest in a long shot. It proved to be successful in the end, but it took a lot of hard work and rehabilitation. The process of recovery certainly did not happen overnight. The day my dad left the hospital, he was stitched, bandaged, and waiting to see what the outcome of the surgery would be.

With my dad's arm bearing a strong resemblance to a patchwork pillow after his surgery, my mom knew he was in no condition to work. It was important that he healed. She worked even harder to get everything done so he wouldn't have to worry about anything. Although she tried to downplay the amount of work she really was doing, my dad was very aware of the amount my mom had taken upon herself. He sat as long as he could and watched until he could no longer stand it. Finally one night he came to the conclusion that, stitches or no stiches, he was not going to sit idle while his wife, who was pregnant with their third child mind you, worked herself sick.

My mom was taking a bath one evening after dinner and my dad slipped out to the garage without telling anyone. He slid behind the little printing press and turned the switch to on. Sitting in a damp and dimly lit garage amongst gas cans and rusted tools, the sound of the machine and the smell of the ink caused his head to feel as if it had floated away from his body for a couple of minutes as the scene of the accident replayed in his mind. He regained his composure, pushed the memories from his consciousness, and began to work.

After just ten minutes, my dad was completely absorbed in his work. His instincts began to take over and he moved quickly and with the kind of expertise that only comes from years of experience. He completely forgot about his arm, the surgery, and the stitches. He focused on his work and thought about his wife and children as he pushed past the initial pain in his arm. After twenty minutes, the pain was replaced by determination. Larry Semprevivo would not let his family down.

While engrossed in the task at hand, my dad did not hear my mom come into the garage. She had realized once she got out of the bathtub that my dad was nowhere to be found, and then heard the commotion in the garage. She knew immediately what was going on. My mom stepped one slippered foot after the next into the garage and quietly stood behind my father with tears rolling down her face. Looking over his shoulder, my mom could see that, on top of the lighted table she used to prepare the fliers, there was a pool of blood. She then looked to the source of the blood. In the midst of working to make the fliers, my dad had broken open several stitches in his arm and hadn't stopped to realize it yet.

My mom knew that his arm had to have been throbbing, but my dad stood stoic and resolved, working harder than ever to make up for the loss of use of his left arm. My mom was never so moved as she was when she saw the level of sacrifice my father was capable of the day she walked in that garage and found him bleeding and working for his family.

CHAPTER FIVE

DISCOVERING THE UNWILD WEST

T ime passed and my parents worked nonstop to find their way back into the working middleclass. It wasn't an easy road either, but none of the kids ever knew that until well into adulthood. There was a point right before I was born that my mom and dad got so desperate they would go out to the countryside where all the farms were and go from door to door asking for fresh eggs, then sell the eggs in town a dollar a dozen just to make ends meet. My dad felt ashamed that they had come to that, that he had to beg for eggs then sell them to others, but it is what he had to do to keep shoes on everyone's feet, food in his children's stomachs, and a roof over his family's heads. It wasn't an easy time for my parents, trying to recover from the accident and barely scraping by, but they did everything they could to make certain our family was taken care of and through all their trials, my parents' focus was the security of their children. They never wanted anyone to know that anything was wrong while they worked to regain their financial footing.

Larry Jr. and Palma were already in grade school by this time and able to pick up on tension and anxiety, so my parents had to work hard to be sure that they would never grasp the severity of what was happening. They would skip meals and make excuses as to why they weren't eating to be sure that my siblings were never made to bear the burden of their struggles. They kept smiles on their faces and warmth in our home, even during the worst of times. They also kept with them the hope of something better. That hope was eventually manifested into success.

The business moved from the garage to an actual facility with the help of one of the only people who stuck by us, Joe Iannelli. My dad went to Joe, who was the foreman of a major printing company, and asked if he could start doing work for Joe's printing company. Joe told my dad he would look into it and, true to his word, he did. A sales team came out and inspected the facility that was in Cherry Hill where my family lived, okayed the facility, and my parents were finally feeling that their effort and attitude were being rewarded.

With a new facility and renewed optimism for the future, my parents began to build an impressive repertoire of clients which started with a major investment company who supplied buy-and-sell reports to their clients. These reports were vital; they were what moved Wall Street. They would come to my parents press and need to be out by Saturday morning, so my entire family would help prepare them.

My parents did these reports for some time, but never once did they use the information. Every week they saw what stock would go up and which would go down, but my dad felt that it would be dishonest to use the information, so the only thing he ever did was print it and send it out. Taking care of his family was important to him, but doing so honestly and with integrity was his priority, so instead of taking an easy way out, my dad did what he felt was honorable. He worked long hard hours instead of using information that was under his nose weekly. To him, his integrity was worth much more than his financial success.

The print press continued to grow and so did our family. In 1971 I was born, the bundle of joy that was a product of my dad's new perspective after coming so close to death. I was kind of like a phoenix for my parents. Everything was finally settling down and my family was making a full recovery from the tragedy that happened the year before.

Although my dad's arm was showing signs of improvement, the winters in the northeast could be brutal, and the freezing temperatures were taking their toll on him. The surgery had helped tremendously, but a lot of damage had been done, so cold weather would cause unbearable aches and pains. After six years of harsh winters that were nearly debilitating for my dad, in 1976 my parents finally decided that there was only one answer to their problem, warmer weather. My parents sold everything we had, including the printing business, packed the kids, clothes, and the family dog, and headed west. We were Arizona bound.

It took us an entire month to make our away across the Bible Belt. We left our home in New Jersey in July, and our tires crossed the New Mexico state line in August. For Larry Jr. and Palma, my brother and sister, it was a difficult month; they were leaving their home, their school, and all their friends behind, crammed into a car with four other people and a dog, and spending day after day staring out of a car window.

I, however, was only five years old, so I found the entire thing fascinating. To me, our trek was an adventure. I was seeing new places, eating food I'd never had before, and hearing accents I thought were only used in movies. Among other things, I learned that everything is better when you fry it and how to use y'all in the right context as we made our way from the east coast to the Arizona desert.

While driving through New Mexico, my parents found out that in the west, school starts in August, not September. My mom and dad didn't want us to start school late, so instead of pushing on into Arizona, they decided to settle in New Mexico for the time being. Since we had left without a definite destination, we were afforded some flexibility when it came to laying our roots. My parents' only stipulation was warmer weather, and New Mexico certainly offered that, so my mom and dad began to scout out the cities and towns we drove through, not knowing exactly what they sought, but sure that they would know when they found it.

On a hot August day, our family station wagon rolled into a town by the name of Deming. We strolled through the town and, as we drove, my dad felt drawn to the place. He had never heard of the town, but it felt comfortable and peaceful to him. As I have explained, the accident had stirred within him a new level of spirituality and, after passing at least twenty churches in the fairly small community, my dad felt spiritually moved by the town so he decided this would be the place we would call home—at least for a while.

Not knowing anything about the town, my parents set out immediately to find a place to live for the time being. It isn't easy to start over. It is particularly difficult to do so when you haven't a single acquaintance and have never been to the state in which you are beginning anew. We had each other, though, and that was all we needed. My parents soon found a place called the Christ Living Center, which was a cylinder block building with linoleum flooring throughout the entire complex. It was nothing fancy, but it would be a roof over our heads as my parents planned what to do next. We spent the next months adjusting to the new town in our 700 square foot abode.

Something that my family noticed instantly as we began to re-establish ourselves in a part of the country we knew nothing about was that there were not many other Italian families around. In fact, there was not a single Italian in the entire town until we moved in.

Often times, when one thinks of the United States, the melting pot metaphor comes to mind. It was clear, however, that, although we may have been in the same pot, we were not welcome ingredients in the southwest. Our family may as well have been from outer space. The locals either had preconceived notions that were built from stereotypes of both easterners and Italians, or they had no idea what we stood for, so they just assumed the worst. We dressed differently, talked differently, and lived differently.

For the first time, my parents and siblings experienced a real dose of culture shock. The list of differences between New Jersey and New Mexico seemed endless. Perhaps the biggest dissimilarity between the northeast and the southwest is in the way time is treated. My parents were used to the fast pace of the urban northeast. It seemed to them that New Mexicans didn't take their cues from the clock. They moved slow, talked slow, and did business slow. Nothing went quickly in the west. It seemed no one ever had to be anywhere. My dad first learned this standing in line at a bank waiting to open an account in their new hometown.

"Well thanks, Lydia," a tall lanky man in a straw hat, decked out in denim from head to toe said to the teller, as she stood behind the desk, smiling from behind her giant, mauve glasses.

"Not a problem at all, Mr. Johnson. Say, how's the ranch going? Your calves doing well? I heard the coyotes are terrible in some places," the teller replied, leaning onto one hand as she settled into her conversation with the cowboy.

"You know, I've lost a couple, but it ain't no worse than last year. Got some good momma cows and a mean mule out there. They usually keep those coyotes in their place. I think it'll be a good year as long as it don't dry up too bad and burn the pasture up," the lanky, bronze skinned cowboy said, shifting his weight from one booted foot to the other.

My dad stood patiently behind the man as he went on to tell about the problems his neighbor had had with his cattle. He was as amused as he was bewildered. He looked around, waiting for Clint Eastwood to appear in the bank at any moment, cloaked in a poncho with his sweat stained hat pulled down over his eyes.

After a week in Deming, my parents felt as if they hadn't traveled across the United States, but that they had traveled back in time. Time really did move slower in the west, of that there was no doubt. Although it was a bit odd at first, there was something really quaint about it that both my mom and dad liked. Sure, it would take some time to adjust to, but there weren't really any good reasons either of my parents could think of not to slow down. Life had a way of becoming hectic and using schedules and deadlines to control every moment of the day, but the west had found a way to break that cycle and my parents figured they may as well take advantage of their break from the present. So this was Deming, New Mexico. . .

⎯⎯⎯⎯⎯⎯⎯

CHAPTER SIX

ANOTHER SPEED BUMP

M oving from New Jersey to New Mexico was not easy for everyone in my family. Larry Jr. and Palma particularly struggled with it. I was too young to be too affected by the experience and, as I had said, I saw it as an adventure and thought the desert and cowboys that surrounded us a novelty. My brother and sister, being so much older, didn't appreciate the uniqueness of our new home as much as I. My parents were sensitive to this fact and began to do all they could to make life pleasant while Larry Jr. and Palma found their desert legs.

Eventually, my parents bought a fifteen acre tract of land at the foot of the Florida mountains out in the middle of nowhere. Our land was surrounded by Bureau of Land Management government land, so we were somewhat secluded.

With the money left from the profit on selling the house in Cherry Hill, my parents built a house on the land that was big enough to accommodate our entire family. We finally had our own home. Along with building a house to start reestablishing security for me and my siblings, my parents also began to do things like kick ball Sundays and make sure that we all sat down for every meal together when we could. My dad even bought all of us kids animals to be our pets and to teach us responsibility. We had horses, goats, and chickens; we were turning into a real farm out there on those fifteen acres. If only the folks back in New Jersey could see us now.

Living out in the country with our closest neighbors at least a mile away, we became a very close-knit family. We had always been a close family, but being in a foreign place with no friends or family outside ourselves, our family grew even stronger. We all began to realize how important family was; that it was the backbone of our existence and that, as long as we had had one another, we could do anything.

Although we did spend a short stint quite isolated from the rest of the town, it was only a matter of time before we all finally branched off of our little piece of the world and began to thrive within the community. The people were, like I said, a little leery of the Italian family from the east that talked funny and kept to themselves but, as we reached out to the people of Deming, they reached back.

Larry Jr. and Palma began to make friends at school and my dad became involved in everything he could, from working for the volunteer sheriff department to becoming a member of the Knights of Columbus. All this, combined with our family joining the Catholic Church in town, allowed us to shift from the awkward outsiders to a part of the community. As soon as we made the first move and let people into our lives, we realized that it wasn't that people didn't like us, they just didn't know anything about us. Once they did, though, they were more than happy to welcome the first Italian family in Deming.

Just as things were smoothing out, however, we hit yet another hiccup. Two years into becoming permanent residents of Deming in the fall of 1978, my dad suddenly fell ill. It was strange, because it seemed to come out of nowhere.

On a brisk fall evening, my mom made homemade chili for our family to mark the beginning of the autumn season. Shortly after eating, my dad became violently ill. He began to vomit, broke out in a cold sweat, and the pigment seemed to fade from his skin, leaving him a very unnatural pale gray. At first, my dad assumed it was the chili that had done this to him, but after an entire day of intense pain without any kind of relief and no one else in my family reacting to mom's cooking, he realized that something worse than a bowl of ground beef and ranch style beans was at the root of this.

"Hon, I'm going to need you to take me to the hospital," my dad said to my mom from between clenched teeth as he fought back nausea and the tried to ignore the excruciating pain in his abdomen.

"Come on kids. Get your stuff together now and get to the car," my mom sprung to action immediately and helped my dad out to the black Cadillac that sat in our drive.

The car stayed completely quiet as we drove. That was becoming a theme, it seemed, for my family; intense, quiet car rides. My dad gripped his stomach as we made our way down the road into town. Sweat beaded across his forehead and soaked his shirt as we drove. We hardly ever saw our dad in such a vulnerable state, so all three of us sat in the back seat awe struck by the whole thing. We knew, because vulnerability was not on the long list of traits my father possessed, that this was serious.

My mom pulled into the emergency parking area and a hospital employee came to help my dad from the passenger side of his own car to a wheel chair. Our family followed close behind as my dad was wheeled into the large brick building with automatic doors that opened as we approached. If this scene sounds somewhat familiar, it's because it is. This was not the first time my dad had passed through hospital doors without any idea of what the outcome would be.

My mom went straight to the admittance desk where a woman with too much makeup and perfume so strong that I could smell it from where I stood sat staring blankly back at my family.

"My husband needs to see a doctor right away," my mom said, looking around the room to see where she should take my dad.

Without saying a word, the woman turned to a filing cabinet, then turned back to us and slammed a stack of papers in front of my mom.

"You'll need to fill these out and then we can get him back to see a doctor," she said without any emotion in her voice at all, as if we were there to get the oil in our car changed.

My mom looked over at my dad, who was still grimacing in pain and becoming more pale by the minute, then back to the stack of papers.

"Please, take my husband back to see a doctor and I'll get these filled out as he is being treated," my mom pleaded with the woman.

"This is hospital policy and you must complete all the pages in order for your husband to be brought back for any diagnostic tests or treatment."

"What if he's having a heart attack?!" my mom asked, her words wrapped with disbelief as the irony of this place being called an "emergency room" hit her hard; a misnomer to say the least.

"Doesn't matter, it's still policy," the woman replied, either unaware of my mother's desperation or just apathetic to it. Apparently this woman didn't have loved ones of her own, or she had just become completely detached from the reality that the people who come through her admittance line weren't extra work, they were human beings.

"When the paper work is finished," the woman said staring straight at my mom, "he can go back."

When the woman finished her sentence, she turned away from my mother and went about her business. This was just another day for her. As my dad sat beside my mom, becoming worse while the clerk explained hospital policy, the woman never once even looked over at him.

My mom realized that arguing would get her nowhere, so she took the stack of papers and began to rush through them as quickly as she could. She handed the papers back to the clerk, and finally a doctor came to take my dad back to a room. He looked like he was on the verge of death by the time they got to him. He had turned pale grey, almost white, and was nearly lifeless.

As the doctor disappeared around the corner with my dad, the clerk looked back up at my mother, who stood and stared back apprehensively to where the doctor had taken my dad.

"I'll need your driver's license," she said flatly.

My mom produced her license and handed it to the frosty clerk. The woman took my mom's information down, then handed it back.

"I need your husband's as well," she said.

"I don't have his. His license is with him," my mom explained.

"We can't do anything for him without his license. You need to go get it from him if you don't have it."

"I have no idea where they've taken him," my mom answered, still in shock by the insolence of the woman.

"Look around the corner," was the only kind of help the clerk offered in response.

My mom went back and found my dad, got his license, and brought it back to the ill-mannered clerk. With all his paperwork up to par, my dad was in the emergency room for a few hours while doctors checked basic vitals, then did blood work to finally discover that it was the gallbladder that was causing the pain. My mom's cooking was off the hook.

My mom, grandma, and I passed the time in the waiting room from around seven in the morning until two in the afternoon. My brother and sister had gone to school because their school was walking distance from the hospital, but mine was further away, so I stayed with my mom and waited.

After finding out that it was my dad's gallbladder, they moved my dad into a semi-private room since he would have to stay for a surgery. His roommate was a man who was suffering from bleeding ulcers. Doctors were in and out with the man all night, which meant my dad was up all night as well.

After a sleepless night, two doctors wheeled my dad into the operating room and told my mom and grandmother that this was a fairly simple procedure and they would let them know when they were finished.

After more time passed than seemed necessary for a simple procedure, one of the doctors emerged from the operating room and approached my mom and grandma. They had been pacing the halls in front of my dad's room as they waited. The expression on the doctor's face sent alarms off inside my mother. She had seen these kinds of expressions before; they were the kinds of expressions that wheel your husband into a snow filled parking lot and walk away.

"We did the best we could," the doctor started, "but there were some complications. When the gall bladder was removed, it had to be peeled off the liver. We don't know what the outcome will be, but you should prepare for the worst. He is bleeding internally. We don't think he is going to make it."

Don't think he is going to make it penetrated deep in my mother's eardrums and rattled around inside her head. She and my grandma both began to cry, falling into each other's arms. How in the world had this happened? He was fine a day ago. The procedure should've been simple enough. None of it made sense. This was my mom's worst nightmare; to lose the man she adored and depended on. It wasn't that she needed him to get by or to help raise us, but she needed him to survive. He wasn't just her husband, he was her other half. Without him, my mom was lost. The doctor said to prepare for the worst. There is no way to prepare for losing half your heart.

My mom and grandma sat and waited, not knowing how exactly they should "prepare for the worst." They waited and prayed and cried, until finally the doctor came out and said that the bleeding had stopped and my dad was in recovery. After a little more time, my dad was brought back to his room, now sporting a half inch wide scar that went from his belly button to his sternum. He was in quite a bit of pain, but at least the scar made him look tough, he would go on to say.

The doctors kept my dad in for a week while he recovered from the surgery. A week in a hospital was like a month at a nice hotel where cost was concerned, and the room service isn't even comparable. After my dad was considered well enough to go home, all my parents had to do was come up with money for the bill. My dad no longer had health insurance since he wasn't a Union member and was self-employed, so the expense was the sole responsibility of my parents. Without any other options, my mom emptied the bank account to pay the bill that day. They were now broke, but they were broke together, so they were both content with that. With an empty bank account, my mom and dad left the hospital hand in hand.

⚭

CHAPTER SEVEN

THE DIAGNOSIS

Less than a year after my dad's gallbladder surgery, another serendipitous occasion moved my family a step closer to the ultimate success that would come later. My parents had become friends with our neighbors, the Luscombs, who lived down the road, and they would have dinner or get-togethers occasionally. During one of these get-togethers our neighbors had mentioned how their son Daniel had a great restaurant in Columbus, New Mexico, which was not too far from Deming.

My parents never thought much of the Luscomb boy's restaurant, until one day when they decided to go to a museum in Columbus to see an exhibit my dad was interested in. After visiting the museum, my parents decided to stop in for lunch at Daniel's restaurant. As they were eating lunch, Daniel came over to greet them. My mom and dad instantly liked him.

Daniel was a giant burly guy who had the build of a lineman and the demeanor of a little boy. He stood over six feet tall and must have weighed 400 pounds, but his personable character did not match his overwhelming physique. He was like a giant kid, always smiling, joking, and laughing. His face always seemed to glow with excitement and he possessed an air of innocent naïveté that made you love him the second his mouth opened. This Daniel was certainly a gem. He was quite the chef, too. Along with Daniel's lovable personality, my parents were impressed with the food that day at the restaurant.

That wouldn't be the last time my mom and dad would see Daniel. One evening the Luscombs were having dinner and invited our family to join. Daniel was there as well. As we sat around the Luscombs' dining table and nibbled at green bean casserole and lemon chicken, Daniel began to pitch an investment opportunity to my parents.

"What I really want to do, Mr. and Mrs. Semprevivo, is open a restaurant here in Deming. I think it would be perfect. There's nothing like it here, and it could be the new hotspot in town," Daniel was saying, his eyes wide and shining as he spoke.

"I can definitely see the promise in that," my dad agreed, laying his fork on his plate as he thought about what Daniel was saying. "And the food will sell itself. You are quite a chef, Daniel."

"Why, thank you, Mr. Semprevivo. That means a lot to me. I take a lot of pride in what I do," Daniel responded with a slight rose color rising in his cheeks.

"So, what is it that you think we can do?" my dad cut to the chase.

"Well, I'll need some capital for start up. There would be a building to lease, equipment, supplies; all the stuff to get us off the ground. I know once I get it going, it will fly. I just need some help getting it off the ground."

"What kind of help?" my dad asked, feeling excitement and apprehension deep down in his stomach.

"I would say that fifty thousand would get everything I need to get going," Daniel replied, his eyes glued to my dad's, trying to guess what his reaction might be.

"That's a lot of money," my dad answered, looking to my mom.

"Absolutely, it is," Daniel agreed. "But I know I can do this, Mr. Semprevivo. It's a sure thing."

"Well, I'll talk to my wife, and we'll let you know," my dad said to Daniel, even though he was already almost certain he wanted to be a part of this.

My mom and dad discussed the proposition and weighed the pros and cons. By the end of the discussion, they decided that this sounded like a perfect investment for them. Neither had ever been involved in the restaurant business before, but they were fast learners and they trusted Daniel. There was one thing that stood in their way, however; my mom and dad had spent all of their money to pay for my dad's gallbladder surgery. They thought that this restaurant was a perfect opportunity for them, but they would have to do something to come up with the fifty thousand dollars.

My parents sat and discussed their options, then settled on one. They still had a commercial building on a piece of land back in New Jersey. They would sell that piece of land and use the money to start up the restaurant. So, they sold their last bit of New Jersey and in 1979 my parents went into partnership with the young and charismatic French chef and hoped for the best. As time passed, they only became more confident in their investment. The restaurant was a success and they had finally found their place in Deming, New Mexico.

My parents weren't the only ones who were learning how to be businessmen, however. I had found my niche as well, and my business was foolproof because there was no risk or monetary investment involved. You see, I would go to my parents' restaurant, raid the candy and pretzels, then go to school and sell them to my classmates. Only eight years old and I was already an entrepreneur.

Unfortunately for me, my principal wasn't nearly as impressed with my entrepreneurial spirit as I. Upon realizing what I was doing, he called my parents in to tell them what was going on. He did tell them, though, that I had figured out to wait until the other students were starving to go in for the sale. Perhaps he was a little impressed.

So, my principal outing my sales tactics abruptly ended my stint as a candy and pretzel salesman, but it did not stop me from raiding the candy at my parents' restaurant. You've heard the expression, "I was like a kid in a candy store." Well, that expression is used for good reason, and seeing me in my parents' restaurant shoveling sugary snacks into my school bag was the perfect example of why.

My dad began to worry about the amount of sugar I was eating at the time. Sure, every kid loved sweets, but not every kid had access to them the way I did. At the time, I thought it was paradise. I could go in and grab anything I wanted any time of the day.

What I didn't realize while I was snatching sweets from the restaurant kitchen was that I was doing some real damage with all those chocolate bars, gum drops, and gobs of taffy. I would find this out in a very strange way, too.

One morning while reading the Deming Headlight, I came across an article that was about a bikeathon. That sounds awesome, I thought as I began to read on to find out how to register. As I read about the race, my eyes fell on the purpose of the race; to raise awareness for diabetes. Along with information on how to register, the article provided a list of symptoms for diabetes. I noticed immediately something strange about the list; I had four of the eight symptoms.

I told my mom about the article and the symptoms I had. She wasted no time in getting me to our family doctor. After some blood work and a couple of questionnaires, a doctor pulled my parents aside and told them that I was, in fact, diabetic. This was in 1980, and medicine hadn't come as far as it has today in the understanding and care for diabetes.

I want you all to sit down," the doctor said, as my parents walked into the room. It's never going to be good news that follows such a statement. My dad took my mom's hand into his own and they sat, waiting for what would come next.

"Joseph's results came back and he does have diabetes," the doctor said, annunciating every word to be sure that he was understood.

"What does that mean, then, doctor," my mother asked, fighting back tears. "What do we do now for Joseph?"

"Well, it means a lot. One, he will have to change his lifestyle completely. No sugar at all; his diet will have to be very strict. He'll also have to be on medication from this point on. He'll need insulin, so you and your husband will have to learn to give Joseph shots."

"Okay. We can do that. No sugar and insulin. We can do that," my mom said, sitting with her legs tightly crossed at the ankles, steadying herself on the edge of the hard plastic chair in which she sat.

"There's more, though, and I don't know how to make it less painful," the doctor said, staring straight into my mother's eyes, and then to my father's.

"This is not an easy disease and it affects a lot."

"We understand," my dad broke in. "We're going to make sure he doesn't eat sugar and that he gets his medicine."

"No," the doctor said right as my dad finished, "it's more difficult than that. Joseph will probably only live to twenty-one, if even that. This disease is just too hard to control."

My mom burst into tears and my dad sat in silence, shocked by what the doctor had just told them. I was waiting for my parents in the doctor's office the entire time this was going on. After some time, my mom and dad rounded the corner to come and get me to take me home and, as they did, they both dried their eyes and smiled before I could see that they were upset.

"You ready, buddy?" my dad asked, as he patted me on the back.

"Yup!" I replied. "What did the doctor say, dad?"

"We'll talk about it at home, kiddo. Don't worry; it's nothing we can't handle," my dad said as we walked out the doors to our car.

I believed my dad when he told me that, because he was right; as long as I set my mind to it, there was nothing that I couldn't handle, especially with the support system I had behind me.

Both my parents were scared to death when they heard my diagnosis, but they would not let it beat them and they would not let it beat me. After discussing it, they decided to take me to a clinic in Boston that specialized in diabetes to be sure I got the best care and that they did everything they could to defeat the prognosis the first doctor had given us. We packed up what we needed and headed out back towards the great northeast to see what could be done.

CHAPTER EIGHT

FROM RESTAURANT TO RUIN

We were in Boston for a couple of weeks while doctors worked to see what I would need to do to overcome what basically was a death sentence. While we were there, my parents closed down the restaurant for the time being, but had every intention of reopening once we were back in town. When we returned home, however, my parents put the restaurant up for sale because the closest major hospital was in Las Cruces. They wanted to be sure that we were close to a hospital in case of an emergency. My parents had worked hard on their business, but when it came between the restaurant and my health, there wasn't even a question; we would move to Las Cruces to be close to a hospital.

The restaurant sat on the market for only a short time and as soon as it was sold we were on our way to Las Cruces. My parents knew that this move meant that they were essentially starting over again and it may be tough, but they would be sure that I never knew how tough and, above all else, they would be sure I beat the odds, even if that meant moving.

Now that my parents had some experience in the restaurant business, they decided to give it a go a second time in our new home of Las Cruces. They bought a small place and did a little fixing up and were soon the proud owners of Caesar's Italian Restaurant. After some time and success with Caesar's, my parents decided to sell and build a larger restaurant. The second restaurant fell in suit with the others and did great.

Years passed and nothing out of the ordinary happened to our family. Things finally seemed to be going smoothly for us. We had a solid family business, I was getting the medicine and treatment I needed for my diabetes and, although we still hadn't been able to sell our old house back in Deming, we did have tenants there whose rent helped go toward our family bills. Unfortunately, this was just the calm before the storm.

After years of hard work with only one trip—the trip to Boston to see a diabetes specialist for me—my parents decided that the family was probably due for a vacation. We had all worked hard and we deserved to get away from Las Cruces, from the restaurant, and from our daily responsibilities. There was a manager to watch over things in their absence, so they figured there was nothing standing in the way. They had no idea the long awaited trip would cost much more than airfare and hotel expenses.

After the vacation my parents arrived home to a nightmare. Just two weeks prior, they had left a thriving restaurant that showed a lot of promise. They returned to an AWOL manager and zero money. The man they had trusted to keep things in order while they were gone had embezzled every last penny and took off. That crooked manager didn't just steal money when he skipped town, he stole my parents' dreams, erased their hopes, and demolished their hard work. They had put years into that restaurant. It was their present and their future.

This was not going to be easy to recover from, but a restaurant run into the ground wasn't the first hardship they had faced. It wouldn't be the last, either, so they did what my parents always do and they kept fighting. They knew that wallowing in self-pity or throwing in the towel wouldn't do anyone any good, so they brushed the betrayal off and got to work. Hard work and having the support of an amazing family to keep you going can take you a long way after all, even when things are looking pretty grim.

My parents tried to recover from the massive losses, but it just could not be done. The embezzler who had destroyed years of work had done too much damage so bankruptcy was their only choice. My parents reluctantly went through the bankruptcy process and knew immediately that we would not be able to stay in Las Cruces now that everything was gone. We each packed up our own rooms as we prepared to return to Deming. Deming wasn't a bad place to return to—we still had friends there and it was familiar. The reason that we were returning made it feel as if we were headed off to fulfill a prison sentence. We were being punished for some crime that we couldn't put our fingers on and no one could define, but we had to pay for it nonetheless.

We got the car loaded and once again we were off. As we drove down the oil stained highway that was engulfed by heat and miles of desert, we hit yet another snag; our car broke down. We were the very definition of stranded.

We all sat on the side of the road until someone finally stopped to help. We loaded into the helpful stranger's car and he took my dad to the nearest dealership, then dropped us off at home. My dad had to get a tow truck to go out to the car, so he rode with the tow truck driver out to where our family car had croaked, and then back home. Once the car was safe in our driveway, its battery died completely, so we were stranded at our house for two days. That doesn't seem like a long time, but when you know you have no way to get anywhere and you are in a rural area without any nearby neighbors, two days feels like a lot like eternity. Finally on the third day, my dad walked a mile down our rough dirt road to a neighbor's so he could get a ride to the dealership yet again to get a battery for the broken down car.

Without even enough money to pay for the sixty dollar battery, my dad had to make a deal with the auto dealer that he would pay the battery off in installments. Years of working hard and putting countless hours in his own business and there he was negotiating payment plans for a sixty dollar battery with a used car salesman. As he walked away with the new battery in hand and calculations of how much to pay and how often running through his head, it occurred to my dad that this may have been his low point. He had been through a lot and come out on the other side, but this time he wondered if he would be able to pick himself up and dust himself off as he had with everything else.

The battery ordeal wasn't the only problem we faced upon returning to Deming, either. As we pulled into the drive of our old house, my dad's nightmare only continued. The previous occupants had been less than ideal renters while in the house. The place was destroyed; yet another obstacle for my family to overcome.

We had nothing to fall back on this time; there was no home or real estate back in New Jersey to sell. Each previous instance that we felt like we were in the middle of the ocean about to drown, there was always a life preserver for us to swim to. This time we were going to have to use our own strength to get to shore. All our life preservers had been used up.

With my family suffering one blow after another, my dad had lost his optimism and his unbreakable will was beginning to finally crack. There we were, back in Deming in a thrashed house with no savings and not even enough money to buy a battery for a car. My dad wasn't terribly concerned about the battery though. What he worried about more than repairing cars, paying electric bills, or coming up with the money to begin a new restaurant, was me. I needed insulin to live and without money there was no possibility I would get the medication I needed. This was bigger than my dad's pride or having to settle into a new social class; this was life or death for me.

As my dad sat one day in the living room, the inventory of devastating blows my family had received piled down on him hard. He thought about how much money they needed, then about how much they didn't have. He thought about me and my insulin, and about my mom, Palma, and Larry Jr., too.

They may have not needed medicine, but they would need to eat and need shoes on their feet. As he considered all these things, he began to feel as desperate as he did the day he was caught in the printing press feeder. Once again there was no one to push the emergency shut off button.

As my dad sat contemplating where he was at that moment in time and what all that meant to his family, my mom walked into the room. She could tell by the expression on my dad's face and the anxiety in his eyes that he was agitated.

"Hey there, Lar. Why the face?" my mom asked as she came to sit beside my dad in the quiet living room.

"It's the money, Jo. It's everything else, too, but it all comes back to the money. I have no idea how we are going to make it. I am fifty years old and starting from scratch," my dad said with real fear in his voice.

"Let me ask you something, Lawrence Semprevivo," my mom started with force, but also with love. "Have you always made money for this family?"

My dad paused, taken back by both my mom's question and the resolve in her words. She was so sure of him, so certain of what she said. He was on the verge of a breakdown, but not my mom. She knew that they would be okay and she made him realize that too.

"Yeah," my dad replied, realizing the weight in his answer as it escaped his lips. There was a lot of power in that one word, "yeah." "Yeah I have."

"Then get yourself up and go make more, Larry. That's all there is to do. Quit sitting in this house feeling sorry for yourself and find a new path."

How simple, my dad thought as my mom finished. *Just find a new path. Of course! Sitting here is not digging me out of any hole.*

Again, my mother's strength carried my dad out of a place of despair and back to his old hopeful self. Again she picked him up off the ground when he had fallen and brushed him off. She was always there to pick him up when he needed it the most.

So with a newfound optimism and my mom as his number one fan and forever supporter, my dad went out and got a job as a cook for a nearby hotel to make more money. He wasn't the only one to do so. My mom got a job as a hostess at the same hotel restaurant and Larry Jr. got not one, but two jobs with two different restaurants and so began the rebuilding process. It was entirely a family effort and not one person ever grumbled about the seemingly nonstop work. We all knew what had to be done, so we did it and we did so without complaint.

For months my mom, dad, and big brother worked to get my family back on its feet. They were relentless in their determination. As always my mom and dad kept our happiness and security in mind as they built something out of nothing. They were doing this for us, after all.

Even though she was working, my mom was still a stickler about making family meals and sitting down together when we could. The only difference now was my mom didn't always eat when she joined us. She would sit down and make us each a plate, ask how our days had gone, and tell us what she had done for the day.

"Dinner's ready, "my mom would call into the living room, the backyard, or wherever I might have been at the time.

"Hi, mom!" I would say as I came stomping through the house toward the table.

"All right, everyone take their places," my mom instructed as she portioned out lentils and pasta.

"Aren't you going to eat with us, mom?" I asked one time when I noticed there was no plate for her.

"I already did while you were out messing around, kiddo," my mom replied with a smile as she ran her fingers through my messy hair.

My mom seemed to do that a lot at that time—eat while we were out playing or watching TV in the next room. I thought she must've just been too hungry to wait on us.

What I found out as an adult is that she wasn't skipping our family dinner because she had been too impatient to wait; she wasn't eating anything at all to make sure that none of us left the table without full stomachs. If there was enough left on our plates after we pushed ourselves from the table and pranced off to watch some more TV or do our homework, my mom would eat what was left. If we cleaned our plates, my mom would skip the meal and wait for breakfast. She went without food to make sure we never had to. She went without food to make sure that we would never know how hard things were. In secretly skipping meals my mother didn't just let me have a second helping if I wanted, she let me stay kid a little longer.

Eventually the hard work and nights without dinner finally paid off. With both my mom and dad working and Larry Jr. giving every penny he made to our family we slowly immerged from the ashes of the bankruptcy.

After four months working, saving, and sometimes starving, my mom and dad had enough money to rent a little abandoned restaurant in Deming. The owner of the place let them do a rent to own contract on it so they could get the restaurant going even though they didn't have quite enough to buy the place yet. After paying first month's rent, my parents got the utilities turned on, bought supplies, and did the fixing up that was needed to open the doors of Larry's Italian Restaurant. They were, once again, headed in the right direction all because of the dedication that my parents and brother had to overcoming our circumstances.

As opening day grew near, everyone was excited about my family's triumphant return to the restaurant industry. We had all played a role in getting the place ready and we were all going to help out as the restaurant got off the ground. My mom would be Larry's Italian Restaurant's only hostess and waitress, Palma would be the cashier, my dad would be the cook, and I was proud to be the dishwasher and my dad's right-hand man. We were set with our tasks and ready to go. What I haven't mentioned yet is that Palma was pregnant at this time—nine months pregnant. And also that she had the baby the day before grand opening. So, I guess I should say that most of us were ready for the opening, anyway.

Opening day came and the little ten table restaurant unlocked the doors and welcomed its first customers. My parents had decided that my mom would just have to wear three hats that night since Palma just had her baby. What was one more thing, right?

Just as it was almost time to open the doors for Larry's debut, in walked Palma, baby on her arm and ready to go.

"What are you doing here, Palma?" my dad asked in complete shock that his daughter was actually standing in front of him with a newborn in tow.

"I'm here to work, dad," Palma said plainly.

"You're what? You can't work, Palma. You just had a baby!" my dad was a little stunned but completely moved by my sister's loyalty.

"I said I would work the register dad. That is what I'm here to do. We'll be fine. Now get to the kitchen where you belong," Palma said as she settled into her place at the counter and put the baby carrier by her side. She had my mom's heart.

The opening of Larry's Italian Restaurant was not simply the beginning of a new family business; it was proof of the resilience and spirit of my entire family. That restaurant showed what we were all made of and what we were capable of doing as a team. My dad's ability to overcome, my mom's sacrifice, my brother's nonstop working, and my sister's dedication all went into the opening of that restaurant. Larry's Italian Restaurant was the manifestation of hard work and persistence.

CHAPTER NINE

FROM COLD TO BATTER

"Joseph, what in the world are you doing? You can't eat ice cream. You're going to kill yourself!" my mom said as I walked into the kitchen, my face smeared with strawberry ice cream.

"No, it's fine, ma. I made it without sugar. It's okay if I eat it," I replied, wiping my face with the back of my hand and licking the ice cream away that my tongue was not able to reach.

"You did what?" my mom asked, still concerned with the fact that I was on a death mission fueled by frosty treats.

"I made my own ice cream without sugar with the ice cream maker so I could eat it. It's ice cream for people with diabetes!" I answered excitedly.

In a small apartment off the house, my parents had an ice cream maker that I had learned to use to make ice cream for Larry's. Day after day I would make ice cream that I couldn't even taste because of the sugar, so one day I decided to try something out. I made a mixture with no sugar and used fruit to sweeten the ice

71

cream. As soon as it was ready, I shoved my spoon in the invention to taste what I had made. It was delicious.

After a few spoonfuls of my new ice cream I had to share the news with my parents. This was huge! It was the first time I'd been able to eat a dessert in ages. I didn't even take the time to wipe my mouth before I busted into the kitchen.

After explaining to my mom and dad that I had come up with a way to make ice cream without the sugar, I offered them a sample of my culinary breakthrough. They agreed; it was delicious.

The only problem with ice cream is that when it was frozen it was like a block of ice. Realizing there was work to be done, my dad immediately began to tweak and fine tune the mixture until he had finally gotten it just right. After my dad's adjustments (he not only modified the ice cream so it would freeze properly, but also used all fresh ingredients and made different flavors), we were ready to bring my ice cream innovation to the public. It looked like my candy and pretzel selling days in grade school would not be my last brush with entrepreneurship. My old principal probably could've predicted this one.

As we worked with the mixture and began to make more ice cream, my dad moved the ice cream maker from the house to the restaurant. That meant that every day after school you could find me in the back at Larry's making my special ice cream then putting them in pint containers to take to local businesses. My dad and I would fill pint after pint, then load the ice cream into a minivan and travel from place to place introducing skeptical store owners to Joseph's Sugar-Free Ice Cream.

It took only tasting our frozen invention for most of the store owners to jump at the chance to sell it in their establishments. We were officially on our way to something big. It wasn't only the first sugar free ice cream; it was actually a delicious sugar free ice cream.

As we saw that the ice cream was going to be more than something I made for my own enjoyment, my dad sold Larry's Italian Restaurant and began to focus on our new endeavor. Palma eventually bought her own ice cream and sandwich shop in which we sold the ice cream and were getting new clients all the time. Neither of my parents could've imagined in 1980 when doctors told them that I was diabetic that my diagnosis would lead to something amazing, but there we were years later selling the only sugar free ice cream on the market. Fate is funny like that.

Sometimes things burn hot in the beginning but quickly fizzle out. That was not the case with my new diabetic friendly treat. My ice cream was being picked up everywhere. Slowly, we made our way outward, leaving Deming for surrounding cities, then surrounding cities for further cities, until we eventually spilled over the New Mexico State line. We worked our way into 197 stores. My life had become ice cream. On weekends we did demos and during the week I was at the shop pumping out pint after pint of ice cream into cardboard containers with my face on them. I wasn't even old enough to drive yet, but I had my own little ice cream dynasty. I was on top of the world... until an electrical glitch would stop me in my tracks.

One particular week our sugar free success was almost ripped from us within a three day period. One of our customer's freezers broke down and in the amount of time it took for it to come back on one thousand pints of ice cream were ruined. This was a devastating blow, but I had learned a lot from watching my parents handle life so I didn't let it get me down; I simply worked harder to get another thousand pints to the store, only to have those ruined by another power outage. If your keeping track, that's two thousand pints in a matter of three days. No one can laugh at that kind of loss, but a person can learn from it and I did.

After seeing how unpredictable the ice cream business could be, not because of the stock market or consumer reports, but because of the nature of the product and its dependence on working freezers, I decided that there may be a better way for me and my fellow diabetics to satisfy our sweet teeth.

"What about cookies" I asked my dad after the second ice cream mishap.

"What do you mean?" he asked, assessing the damage.

"I haven't had a cookie in a really long time and I would love a cookie. What if we did sugar free cookies instead?" I asked with visions of sugar cookies tap dancing through my head.

"Well, cookies can't melt. That's a definite plus," my dad replied, mulling over the idea. "You might be on to something, Joseph. We'll see what we can do."

My parents did just that one Saturday morning. It was a weekend that I had some actual free time because we had no demo to do anywhere, so I was at a friend's house. I had left in the morning and my parent's told me that they were going to work on making a cookie for me. By 10:00 a.m. I was so eager about my surprise that I found a payphone and called home just to see how things were going.

"Hello," I heard my mom say on the other end of the line.

"Hey, ma, it's me," I said.

"Joseph? What are you doing? Shouldn't you be off having fun with your friend? What's wrong?" my mom asked with a twinge of apprehension in her voice. When you have a diabetic son, unexpected phone calls can be unnerving.

"I'm just calling to see what you guys are doing. I'm okay," I assured my mom.

"I see," my mom said with a more relaxed tone. "Well, we have a surprise for you when you get home."

"It's ready now?!" I blurted into the phone.

"Yes sir," my mom answered.

"I'll be home soon, ma!" I said hanging up the receiver, not even waiting for a response.

I immediately told my friend that I needed to go home because my parents had made me a special cookie. To a normal teenage boy, it may seem strange to be so excited about a cookie, but to a kid with diabetes, eating a cookie was like walking on the moon. It was something I thought I would never do again for the rest of my life. This was huge for me.

Whether or not they understood my enthusiasm for something as simple as a cookie, my friend's parents took me back home. I ran all the way up our drive and burst in the front door.

"Where is it?!" I panted as I sprinted to the kitchen.

My mom handed me an oatmeal cookie. I looked at it and took my first bite. It was absolutely amazing. As I chewed the first cookie that had touched my lips in seven years, tears pooled in the corners of my eyes and rolled down my face. I was walking on the moon. This was one small taste for me; one giant bite for all diabetics. It was time for the Semprevivos to move on to cookies.

⸺⟨o/o/o⟩⸺

CHAPTER TEN

FORTUNATE COOKIE

Three years after churning out our first sugar free ice cream batch, we were moving on to conquer the cookie world. On the back side of Palma's ice cream store there was a tiny little add-on that we used for our cookie headquarters. We spent hours crammed in the makeshift factory using a melon baller to scoop wads of cookie dough onto large silver sheets covered in parchment paper. We were building our own empire slowly but surely forty-eight cookies at a time.

As we pumped out more cookies and made new flavors, we eventually decided to shift entirely from ice cream to cookies. They were much easier to store and transport and just as delicious as the ice cream. It seemed only logical to switch over. We had a lot of current clients from the ice cream who we made the cookie conversion with, then continued our crusade going from store to store, this time with a product that wouldn't melt during a demo. The decision to change focus to cookies looked like a good one; by the end of 1987 we had sold $20,000 worth of cookies. Not bad for a guy who had just received his driver's permit that year.

Although the cookie business was doing well, it was by no means at the point that it could support an entire family. At fifteen I thought that $20,000 was quite impressive and for a teenager, it certainly was. For an entire family that included a child with diabetes, however, it just wasn't enough. There were supplies to buy, utilities to pay for, gas for traveling from demo to demo. They say you have to spend money to make money and that isn't easy when there isn't much to begin with. My mom and dad knew that they were going to need a little help to keep the cookie company going; they just didn't have any idea where the help may come from. They would've never imagined that it was going to come the way it did, either.

As we were sweating away in a small cookie factory elbow deep in batter, an entire Hollywood crew was traveling from California all the way to the small town of Deming to make a film. The thing about all people—even movie stars—is they have to eat. Once that large crew landed in the dusty little town and settled down, they were hungry. Luckily for them there was a guy by the name of Larry Semprevivo who had been known for his couple of local restaurants that served amazing food. A fellow by the name of Paul Smith, who happened to be the star of the little production, caught wind of this amazing cook named Semprevivo and asked him if he would mind catering the film's meals for them. My dad didn't hesitate to accept the offer and suddenly our little cookie company had some money coming in to help take care of all the odds and ends that were threatening to shut us down.

Along with providing the money to keep us afloat during our humble beginnings, my dad's catering gig also won him a trip out to Los Angeles to visit Paramount pictures, at which time my dad brought plenty of cookies to hand out to anyone he could. Joseph's Lite Cookies had made their way to Hollywood and were hanging out with the stars.

After the little boost from Hollywood, our cookie company continued to gain steam. We had made our way into grocery stores, health food stores, and nutrition stores; Joseph's Lite Cookies were becoming ubiquitous, at least in our region, and we began to get attention from places we never expected and for reasons we never expected. Although it wasn't Hollywood that came knocking the second time, my father's culinary skills in the kitchen would bring our cookies into the limelight once again the very same year that my parents were invited to Hollywood.

Because our cookies were made initially for diabetics, we obviously couldn't use sugar to bake them. The best thing about a cookie is its sweetness though, so my dad had to find something to add sweetness that wouldn't send me or anyone else with diabetes into a coma. What he found to add sweetness was a substance called crystalline fructose which was produced by ADM, one of the world's leading agricultural processors.

ADM had crystalline fructose created, but they had problems with it prematurely browning while baking. The product seemed to have a fatal flaw in that it was useless for baking purposes, but that was one of its intended uses. While the research and development team was working to figure out why the crystalline fructose reacted the way it did, my dad was busy using it without any problems at all. He bought shipment after shipment of the sweetener without a single complaint.

Eventually ADM became interested in what my dad was using the seemingly flawed substance for and decided that the only way to figure out what he was doing with their product was to ask.

"Is Lawrence Semprevivo in?" a man's voice asked as my dad picked up the phone in our tiny cookie factory.

"This is he," my dad said into the receiver.

"Good afternoon, Mr. Semprevivo. My name is Carl Reeter. I am with research and development with ADM and we're interested in what it is you are using crystalline fructose for," the man explained to my dad.

"I use it to make sugar free cookies," my dad said back to the man proudly. "It's a family business we started because I have a son with diabetes."

"I see," Mr. Reeter responded. "And you don't have any problem with the product when you bake with it?"

"None at all," my dad assured him.

"Would you mind, Mr. Semprevivo, if I flew out to your factory to see you use the crystalline fructose?"

"Not at all," my dad answered, more than happy to demonstrate how he had perfected the art of sugar free baking.

Carl Reeter arrived in Deming and made his way to our little factory behind the sandwich shop. He immediately wanted to see how my dad used his company's product. He explained the problems that his team was having with the product and said he wanted to see what my dad was doing differently. He had to see firsthand that the product could be used without complications.

When he saw my dad bake with it he was absolutely amazed at how well the crystalline fructose worked. He was so blown away by not only the way in which my dad was able to use the crystalline fructose, but also in the quality of the finished product that he took samples back with him to Illinois so he could show his colleagues what he had found.

A few weeks after Mr. Reeter visited our factory my dad got another phone call requesting that he fly out to ADM to the research and development department and demonstrate how to use crystalline fructose in baking. Our cookies weren't just delicious, they were innovative!

After my dad's two brushes with fame, it was back to business as usual. We weren't just being recognized by research and development teams; we were becoming popular with major chains that couldn't get enough of our cookies. One of our clients was a nationwide nutritional supplement store who was becoming quite the client. Each time they ordered it seemed they wanted more and more cookies, which was a great thing until one day a 2,600 case (that is 31,200 bags) order came in.

Orders are good to a point, but this one was overwhelming. We knew that we didn't have the means to get out that many cookies in the amount of time they wanted it. It was bittersweet since it meant that we had officially reached the next level, but that we were officially unprepared for that level.

We knew that it was physically impossible to do since our current technique of doing every step by hand allowed us to get between 700 and 1,000 cookies made a day. One afternoon as we all sat in the cramped little factory trying to come up with some sort of solution there was a knock at the door.

"Who do you think that is?" my dad asked looking at my mom.

"I have no idea, Lar. I'm not expecting anyone. Especially no one who would stand and knock," my mom replied looking a little confused.

My dad got up from where he was sitting and moved toward the door. He opened up the factory door and took a step back.

"Can I help you?" he asked a man in a beige jumpsuit with an oval name badge stitched to it that read "Steven."

"Are you Lawrence Semprevivo?" the gruff delivery guy asked my dad, squinting as the harsh New Mexico sun harassed his eyes.

"I am," my dad replied.

"Well, I have a confirmation of delivery right here with your name and this address. I'll need you to sign," Steven handed a clipboard to my dad and then disappeared into his truck and returned with a large crate on a two-wheeler.

My dad signed his name as he stood a little dumbfounded in the doorway of the factory. As the delivery truck chugged and clanked away, my dad opened the box. He looked down and what stared back at him was a Champion Automatic Cookie Depositor. What took us an entire day to do this machine could do in about twenty minutes. It removed the bulk of the cookie forming process; it was exactly what we needed to move to the next level, but we had no idea who had sent it or why.

In complete disbelief of what had just happened my dad called Champion to see what was going on and if they had somehow sent this cookie depositor by mistake.

"Champion Customer Service," a man's voice said into the telephone.

"Yes, my name in Lawrence Semprevivo and I think you may have sent me something by mistake," my dad said as he stared down at the mysterious delivery.

"Can you give me the number on your receipt?" the man asked.

"Sure. Let me see," my dad said as he fumbled with the blue piece of paper the delivery man had left him, then read off the series of numbers.

"No, sir. There is no mistake. That was supposed to go to you," the man told my dad.

"I didn't pay for this," my dad explained, completely baffled with what was going on.

"It's been taken care of, Mr. Semprevivo.

Someone did. Enjoy your Champion" the customer service rep said back.

My dad thanked the man and hung up the phone with the kind of look someone wears when they've been told they've won a sweepstakes—all at once he felt shocked, excited and absolutely grateful.

There was no one that any of us could imagine who would have sent us that machine. Even if someone did have the money, they couldn't have known exactly what we needed. We didn't have time to play dentist to this gift horse though; we had a 2,600 case cookie order to fill.

Unfortunately, the enormous cookie order that was such a blessing ended up turning into a complete disaster. The store that ordered the shipment wasn't as eager to pay as they were to sell our cookies. That meant that we produced $50,000 worth of product, but went months without payment. For a small family-owned business $50,000 could be the difference between success and failure.

We had no clue when the order came in that it would be so difficult to receive payment. With every month that passed without compensation, our belts were pulled in a notch and our breath sucked in a bit deeper. Fortunately, the company did eventually pay. Lucky for us, we were no strangers to riding out a storm. The battle we had to fight with the nutritional supplement store didn't overshadow the miracle of the anonymous gift, either. To this day we have no idea who sent us the Champion and to this day I believe that receiving that cookie depositor when we did played a major role in building our company to what it is today. I only wish I knew who to thank.

CHAPTER ELEVEN

MOVING ON UP

W ith a laundry list of clients who were household names, steady orders coming in to fill, and the appearance of the mysterious automatic cookie depositor, the Semprevivo family was officially on its way up. We were rising from every hardship and setback that life had handed us. After the printing press accident, my diabetes diagnosis, a nearly fatal run-in with a bursting gallbladder, and having a business sunk by a manager while on vacation, my family had finally hit calm waters. At a demonstration in Albuquerque, however, the waters would start to get a little rough again.

While in Albuquerque doing a food show, my dad got deathly ill. It was just he and my mom, so my mom took him to the hospital. After being admitted to the hospital, my dad described to his doctor what was going on.

Neither he nor my mom could believe what the doctor's diagnosis was.

"It would appear that you are having a gallbladder attack, Mr. Semprevivo."

"That's impossible," my dad said, dumbfounded by the doctor's suggestion. "My gallbladder was removed."

"Every one of your symptoms suggests a gallbladder attack," the doctor replied as if my dad hadn't just told him that there was no gallbladder to do any attacking.

"I don't have a gallbladder, though. I had it removed because of a gallbladder attack years ago," my dad said again to be sure the doctor understood what he was telling him.

"Let's go ahead and do an ultrasound just to be sure," the doctor suggested.

The ultrasound proved that there was in fact a gallbladder, and it was in fact causing the problem. My dad immediately called the doctor back in Deming to make sure that he hadn't lost his mind and that they had removed his gallbladder. The doctor assured him it had been removed and told him to come back to Deming for treatment. In an intense amount of pain, my dad went from Albuquerque to Las Cruces (because they couldn't make it back to Deming) to find out what was going on.

On returning to his original doctor, it was confirmed for the second time that the gallbladder was still there and it had developed gangrene. My dad is the only man I know who had a gallbladder removed twice.

Although recovering from a second surgery to remove a gallbladder wasn't easy, my dad returned to work as soon as he could. There was no time to waste on being sick or on being angry that a doctor had almost killed him "removing" his gallbladder, but somehow left a damaged gallbladder behind that went on to almost kill him again. He knew that anger and grudges wouldn't do anyone any good so he looked at this incident the same way he had the others; he was alive and that was what mattered.

After recovering enough to work, my dad was back to his old work ethic, always in the factory baking and improving to make a better product. He had revolutionized the snack industry once with the crystalline fructose and he had no intentions of stopping there. In 1989 my dad took our cookies to a new level that was outside of the box even for him. He had created cookies made by a new kind of product that provided some serious health benefits that were catching the attention of more than just diabetics looking for a way to enjoy a sweet snack.

The new and improved cookies caught the eyes of dieticians who pointed out the many health benefits of the Semprevivo cookie making process. The way in which my dad had began to make the cookies removed the starch and left the protein and fiber, making the cookie lower in carbohydrates and high in protein and fiber; it was the healthiest cookie around. One dietician even suggested that the cookies may contain a compound that could help with stress—delicious and calming.

Once the cookies moved from a simple treat for diabetics to a health food that could have some serious benefits, our business saw another growth spurt. The cookies were recognized by the southwest regional director of the Juvenile Diabetes Foundation International (he actually served our cookies to his guests) and by a professional bodybuilder in Las Cruces who sold about six cases of the cookies a week. We were moving upward and outward. We even made it to the White House.

With cookies that benefitted so many Americans in so many ways, we decided that we should send cookies to the White House so the people in Washington could taste the future of cookies. The Presidential treats were sent in cookie jars that we had made from the Indian nation. One of the staffers who tasted the cookies was so impressed that she got in touch with us and wanted us to chat with the advisor to President Bush Sr. Upward and outward.

From this point forward, it seems that there was one major event after another that was happening to both me and my family's cookie business. I was eighteen and still a high school student, so the split life of an entrepreneur and a senior looking forward to college could be a little exhausting. It could also be a lot to keep up with. My dad, although busy, had a bit more time and a lot more insight on what was going on since he was, above all other things, not a teenager who didn't realize that owning a business at eighteen was anything out of the ordinary.

Because my dad had the advantage of being an adult who had experienced quite a bit in his life, I am going to turn the reins over to him to tell the rest of our story. This is, after all, the story of our entire family and I would be nowhere without all of them. I learned from watching my mom and dad what it takes to be successful—it takes hard work, dedication, and an attitude that says "I will not stop no matter what I am faced with." I learned from watching two amazing people who I call mom and dad what it takes to overcome—it takes strength that defies all circumstances and the ability to pick yourself up, dust yourself off, and try harder. Seeing my parents work so hard through every bad hand dealt and coming out on the other side has taught me that with sacrifice, comes success. All these things are lessons my dad has handed down to me. He always pushed me in a loving way to be my greatest.

I have a story I would like to leave you with that helps demonstrate the values and the unconditional love my dad instilled in me as a kid. One day in high school after grades had been released, I took my grades home to my dad and had a C in a class. I was so worried that my dad was going to be upset. With a little apprehension, I handed him my report card and waited for his response. He looked over all my grades and said this:

"I'm only going to ask you one thing; I want you to dig deep and answer it honestly. Tonight when you go to bed, ask yourself, 'did I give school, life, family, and work 100 percent today?' If your answer is no, then wake up and give 100 percent tomorrow. If you gave it 100 percent and you got a C, that is all I care about, but if I know that you didn't give 100 percent and you got a C, that's a different story."

From that point on in my life, I ask that question every night, "Did you give it 100 percent today?" It is a driver to my motivation. From this story and so many others you can see that my dad has played as big a role in my success, the company's success, and the success of our family. I feel like the next part of our story should be told by the man whose lessons I built my life on. It is his story as much as it is mine, after all.

CHAPTER TWELVE

OUR CUPS RUNNETH OVER

Being a father to Palma, Larry Jr., and Joseph and the husband of Josephine Marie has been a blessing to me every day of my life. The day that Josephine and I exchanged vows I knew that my life was going to be nothing short of extraordinary, not because I would have a wildly successful company or because I would go on to meet Hollywood stars and be on television myself, but because I had found the most amazing woman in the world and she had said "yes" when I asked her to do me the honor of spending the rest of her life with me.

When we had Palma, I was amazed by the overwhelming joys that a little girl brings into the world. With the introduction of Lawrence Jr., I was convinced that my life could not be any more fulfilled. I had a beautiful wife who, as it turned out, was as amazing a mother as she was a spouse, and a daughter and son who I was certain had hung the moon. My life was set—that is until the day of the printing press accident.

After having been so close to losing all that I loved, I realized more than ever how much family meant to me and I wanted more of it so I convinced Josephine that although we had thought we were finished having children, we needed another little one to really make our family complete. Joseph absolutely did that. He was conceived in complete love and from the first day I held him in my arms, I have seen that love reflected in him. It sounds strange, but I sometimes look down at my scar covered arm and thank God for it because of all the blessings it has led to. If it weren't for that accident, we would have never had Joseph, never packed up and moved to New Mexico to escape the bitter cold of the northeast, and we would've never stumbled into what is now a multimillion dollar company. God sometimes puts gifts in strange packages, of that I am sure.

The accident was our strange little path to where we were and I knew that. Where I will start on the path is where Joseph left us, at the end of his high school career but at the beginning of his (and our) rise to the top.

By the time Joseph was about ready to graduate from high school, he had accomplished more than most people do in a lifetime. I was so proud of the man that my youngest was becoming. At only eighteen, he had already shown an unstoppable drive and unbelievable work ethic that led to the creation of a company that was growing by the year. I know I may sound like every other father does when talking about their son or daughter, but the fact is I wasn't the only one who was impressed with Joseph's dedication to success.

Joseph has mentioned that we sent the cookies to the White House. What he failed to mention was that shortly thereafter he followed our cookies to the District of Columbia. In the very same year that we had sent our cookies to the nation's leaders, we found out

that our youngest son, the boy who had been conceived
in the wake of my terrible printing press accident, had
been chosen to be the recipient of quite an impressive
award. Joseph was going to make his own trip to
Washington D.C. to receive the American Success
Award in the White House by the President of the
United States. He was national secretary for Vocational
Industrial Clubs of America (VICA) at the time and
the youngest person ever to receive the award.

Joseph was shocked when he found that he was
being bestowed with such an honor, but I knew that
he was destined for such things. Although there was a
little more disbelief on Joseph's side than my own, I will
admit that, even though I couldn't say I was shocked
by the award, I was thoroughly impressed considering
that some of the other recipients included the world
famous country singer George Strait, and George
Shinn, owner of the Charlotte Hornets Basketball
Team. The award was created to pay tribute to the
deserving recipients who had achieved undisputable
career success and whose educational background
had included vocational/technical education courses
and commitment to the values of training, retraining,
and continuing education. My son still had calculus
homework and had never even lived on his own yet
and he was being recognized for his undisputable
career success.

Regardless of the weight of that first award, which
would be the beginning of many more awards to come,
it didn't come as a complete surprise to me. Although
it was most certainly out of the ordinary, I can't say that
it was a complete shock since I had a behind the scenes

look at what my son put into his success. He may have been the youngest to receive the honor, but he definitely deserved it as much as all the recipients before him.

Joseph's passion for our company had always astonished me. From the time he cranked out his first bowl of sugar free ice cream, Joseph had been on a mission to do something great. I watched him from age twelve to age eighteen work tirelessly to get our products to anyone and everyone he could. When other kids were out at the movies or playing video games with friends, Joseph was right by my side in a tiny little factory buried in cookie dough or he was out doing demonstrations all over New Mexico, Arizona, and Texas.

Joseph, not wanting to cut his friends out of his life, did find ways to spend time with friends while working so he wouldn't lose touch with the people who had been close to him throughout childhood. Joseph incorporated his friends into the business so he and his buddies could enjoy weekends together while he kept his focus on work. His best friend, Adrian Gonzales, would even do twelve hour demos with him on the weekends. When we had the health food store order the 2,600 cases for example, Adrian would go up to the factory when Joseph was managing the plant at night and they would bake cookies to get everything out. Those boys would be up there many late nights working away, but they would also have fun putting in the extra hours. They both impressed me immensely with that kind of work ethic at such a young age and in their loyalty to one another. Birds of a feather, as they say.

When we received the letter in the mail that informed us our son would be the recipient of an award that famous singers and professional athletic team owners had been honored with, I didn't think, *How in the world did that happen?* What I thought as my eyes skimmed past each word was, *No one in the world deserves this more.* That was true, too, because I couldn't imagine any other teenager who could give to his family and his business more than Joseph had. He has been and always will be an inspiration to me.

When all this began, our only intentions were to make something that people like my son could enjoy; we only thought of diabetics tasting ice cream or a cookie for the first time in years, or even decades, not of awards or interviews or even a serious business. My son, however, had bigger ideas than that and he pushed until we all shared that dream. His drive was contagious, too. None of us could help but be optimistic and dedicated after watching Joseph pour his heart and soul into what he did so completely. Many will tell you that their parents, grandparents, or an elder who they watched growing up serve as their role models and are the people who shaped who they became as adults. I will tell you that my own son has played a vital role in shaping me.

Because of this, none of the success that he or the company has achieved has been too surprising to me; humbling, yes, but not terribly surprising.

Speaking of successes, after Joseph's White House visit, we seemed to hit one success after the next. Along with receiving awards for the business, we also began to get invitations to television programs asking us to come on their shows to explain our cookies. Our first was the Dolores Lenko show, which was a local show in Las

Cruces. From that point, more awards and television interviews followed. As the awards and interviews grew, so did our company.

Our company's success only grew with time. We had worked hard, traveled extensively, and spent countless hours in that small add-on off of Palma's original shop baking thousands of cookies a day and after years of dedication and hard labor, our work was paying off in a very real way. We got bigger clients with bigger orders, appeared on bigger television programs, and received bigger awards.

It wasn't just the cookie company that was growing and maturing in that time, though. In spring of 1990 Joseph graduated from Deming High School. In the fall of the same year he was off to college at New Mexico State University. Our youngest son was entering the world of college as an entrepreneur who already had a growing company. We probably should have been prepared for his next step in adulthood, but a parent is a parent no matter how successful their kid may have been in the adult world, so Josephine and I were a little saddened when we realized our little boy wasn't so little anymore and that he was moving on. Luckily for us, Joseph wouldn't let anything come before his family or our company, so he may have been moving on in some ways, but he found every way he could to stay as active as ever in our company.

Once he started college, he could no longer help with the production side of the company, but he was certainly not going to abandon our family cookie company at that point, so Joseph took over the sales side of things while Josephine and I focused on production. When our little entrepreneur wasn't in class, he was doing sales in Las Cruces, demonstrations all over New Mexico, Texas, and Arizona, and every week he made the deliveries to all our major clients.

We never had to ask him to do any of the things that he did; Joseph simply did them. When some college freshman may have been out enjoying newfound freedom and going to college parties, our Joseph was planning his next demonstration or dropping off a truckload of cookies to a client and taking new orders.

He worked round the clock it seemed. I sometimes would worry that he was doing too much and spreading himself too thin, but he always assured me that he had it under control. I often times wondered if he ever slept.

With Joseph's continued commitment to the company, things kept running smoothly and our numbers kept getting better. Our company had really hit its stride at that point and it only seemed to be gaining speed. Things were looking pretty good from where I was sitting, but the scenery suddenly changed for the worse during that first year that Joseph went away for school; it had nothing to do with the cookies, though. While we were receiving more and more orders, picking up bigger clients in more states, and beginning to burst from the tiny factory we were in from all the business that was coming in, our family received news that overshadowed all the success and accomplishments that we had achieved.

—◦/◦/◦—

CHAPTER THIRTEEN

MORE MEDICAL MISHAPS

———◦/◦/◦———

Even with all the kids grown, Josephine still loved to do family dinners and get-togethers as often as she possibly could. We were lucky that all our kids were close to us so we could actually do that. The gatherings were always great for everyone. By this time the family had grown, so we were able to enjoy not just our children now, but our grandchildren as well. I didn't know that you could love anything more than your kids, but grandkids taught me something about that, so neither Josephine nor I could get enough of our family gatherings.

During one of our regular family festivities, Jo (which I often call my wife), Larry Jr., Joseph, and I were all enjoying one of the great treats of the southwest: corn on the cob. As we sat around the table gnawing those little kernels off the cob with butter running down the sides of our mouths, we all laughed and talked about what all had gone on throughout the day. Josephine grabbed her second ear of corn and we lovingly teased her a bit about her passion for corn.

After dinner, Jo brewed a pot of decaf so we could sit and chat a little longer before we called it a night. After brewing the coffee, Jo left us at the table, deciding to go to exercise a bit instead of sitting with us and talking some more.

"I think I'll go work out just a little before bed," my wife said as she pulled the coffee cups from the cabinets.

"Really, Jo?" I asked. "You're not gonna sit down with us and talk a little more?"

"No, I don't think I will tonight. I've got a little tummy ache, probably from the corn. I think a little exercise will help," Jo said with a kind of tight expression on her face.

"Okay, hon. We'll be here if you need us," I said, not thinking too much of the whole thing.

Jo's exercising did not help the stomach ache. As the night went on, the pain started to get worse. What first seemed to be the consequence of an extra ear of corn was obviously something much bigger than too much butter and starch. Once the pain got to be more than she could handle, Josephine came in and told me she needed to go to the hospital because the pain in her stomach had gotten so intense. Having my gallbladder flare up not once, but twice, and remembering the seriousness of that mess, I couldn't help but be a little concerned. No one wants to see their wife of all people in so much pain.

The roles had finally swapped and this time it was me driving my wife to the hospital. When we arrived and got Jo checked in, a nurse came in to see what was going on.

"Hello, Mrs. Semprevivo. I'm going to ask you a few questions before the doctor comes in," the nurse said as my wife held her abdomen and winced in pain. "Could you tell me what has brought you in?"

"It's my stomach," Jo said in a voice that I knew meant she was not okay.

"Have you had a bowel movement today?" the nurse asked.

"No," Jo responded in a heavy breath of pain.

The nurse could tell that something was seriously wrong, so she wasted no more time with any more questions and called the doctor who was tending to the emergency room that night to request the first method, which was to clean the bowels out.

They did that, but it didn't help. They tried a more aggressive approach to clear the bowels that involved a stainless steel tank and hose, at which time my wife began to scream in pain.

The entire episode was awful. What my wife described to me sounded like fifteenth century torture techniques. I had watched this woman give birth to my three children and I had never seen her in so much pain. I was almost sure what that nurse was doing went against the Geneva Conventions. Modern medicine didn't seem so modern and I was terrified about what they were doing to my wife, but I was powerless. The feeling was familiar; it was the same feeling of helplessness I had being caught in the printing press and I didn't like it one bit.

Finally, Jo couldn't handle any more of the torture. All of a sudden she let out a deafening belt and jumped off of the table they had her lying on. Once her feet hit the cold linoleum floors she began to run around the table clenching her lower abdomen.

Because she would not lie still while a hose sent high fluids into her body at a pressure that could remove the paint from a house, the nurse told her to go home and see the doctor in the morning. This experience was shaping up to be like so many other hospital experiences we had gone through.

On the nurse's suggestion, Jo and I went home with nothing accomplished and no answer as to why my wife was in so much pain. Several hours after returning home from the hospital, Jo got violent chills and started to tremble. This was absolutely not right and I knew it so I put her back in the car and decided to take her to the Las Cruces hospital instead. My wife needed help and she needed it fast.

We ran into a major problem upon leaving our home, however. We lived in a house out in the middle of nowhere at the base of the mountains. The location was good for privacy and quiet, but terrible in emergency situations, especially when the emergency situation deals with someone who is having intense abdominal pains. See, the only way to get from our secluded home to the Las Cruces hospital was down a washboard dirt road. That road carved up by rain waters and tire tracks made our trip into Las Cruces agony for my wife. With every bump, Josephine let out an ear piercing scream.

A very long and stressful hour and fifteen minutes later, we arrived at the emergency room in Las Cruces. The doctors immediately took Jo to a room and started working on her. By that time she had a high fever, which was not a good sign. I had no clue what was going on. It was my turn to sit and wait, scared beyond belief with what the doctors would come back to tell me.

The doctors did tests and discovered that Josephine had ruptured intestines and peritonitis. None of us knew what any of that meant, really, but I figured that a ruptured anything was bad. I could remember how awful my gallbladder felt and couldn't imagine what Jo must be feeling with ruptured intestines. I also didn't want to imagine what the consequences of having intestines rupture might be. I always knew Jo was the strong one. The fear of losing her really drove that home.

"Hi, Larry," our family doctor said as he approached me in the waiting room. I didn't like the sympathetic tone or what it might mean.

"Hello, doctor. What's going on with my wife?" I asked, terrified of what the answer might be.

"Josephine is very ill, Larry. What she has is very serious," the doctor began to explain as my heart swelled in my throat and I felt my entire body break into a cold sweat. I couldn't even respond; I just shook my head in response. "We are going to do our best to save her, but I can't make any promises at this point."

Wow. That isn't something that you ever want to hear. Jo had told me before how scared she was when she had heard the very same words about me, but I never imagined what it really felt like. She was right, those were the worst words you could ever hear. When a doctor says "I can't make any promises," things come into perspective. What I had to realize after those words were said was I may be leaving a widower. I had never imagined Jo going first; I didn't want to. She was my world. The whole thing was just too much. I didn't know if I could handle waiting. I had entered my worst nightmare.

After over three hours of surgery, the family doctor came out of the operating room.

"It's going to be touch and go from this point forward," he told me—not the most reassuring words, but not the worst thing he could've said either. "We had to do a colostomy and remove twelve feet of her intestines."

The doctor finished explaining the surgery and what to expect for that point forward, then left me sitting shocked in the waiting room. I didn't know what "touch and go" meant exactly, or what to look forward to. All I knew was I wanted to kiss my wife. I wanted to hold her and tell her I would make everything fine because I was her husband and that was my job. I also wanted to do it because I needed to see she was okay. I needed to hear her tell me she was going to be all right. Truth be told, I needed Jo more than she needed me at that time.

Josephine was in the hospital for nine days after her surgery, three of which were spent in the ICU and six in recovery. The fever ended up dropping, the shaking stopped, and my wife was finally able to be discharged with a colostomy bag in tote. I know she wasn't crazy about the colostomy bag, but I was more than happy to take her home with a colostomy by her side because it meant I was getting to take my beautiful wife home with me.

Jo ended up having the colostomy bag for a total of four months while she healed. Every day of those four months I gladly changed that bag for my wife. She always fought me on it, but I insisted. After fearing that I would never be able to kiss her sweet face or smell her hair on the pillow next to mine, changing a colostomy bag didn't seem like a big deal to me in the least. I married a woman whose colostomy bags I would change until the end of time. They don't put stuff like that in wedding vows, but they mean a lot.

Although I was more than willing to do so, I didn't have to change Jo's bags for the rest of our lives. After four months she had done so well that they were able to reverse the colostomy and she could go about her business as usual. She was happy to have her life back to normal and I was just happy to have her. That was an experience I never wanted to face again. Almost losing Jo was much worse than I ever could've imagined.

CHAPTER FOURTEEN

AGAINST ALL ODDS

⟨·/·/·⟩

Josephine had her surgery to get everything back to normal and our little business started bursting at the seams. We had finally outgrown the little makeshift factory on Gold Street, so we bought a 4,000 square foot factory on Silver Street tenable us to operate at the level we needed to. Usually moving from gold to silver is a bad thing, but that wasn't the case for us as we moved into a new factory that was around five times the size of our previous headquarters.

As the company grew and demands got larger, Joseph only became more dedicated to the success of the company. In less than a year, he went on to receive two more awards after his initial American Success Award. My son also received the Senate Productivity Award from Senator Jeff Bingaman, for his outstanding work as a successful business owner. Award letters seemed to start coming more frequently than bills to our house. Along with the awards, Joseph was appointed to Business Advisory Counsel (BAC) for NMSU Business School by Governor Garrey Curuthers, appointed to

Economic Development Commissioner by Governor Richardson for four years and appointment to the Workforce Development Committee by Governor Richardson for two years.

I could hardly stop beaming I was so proud of Joseph. If someone would have told me a decade before when we were sitting in a doctor's office listening to someone tell us our son wouldn't make it to his twenties that something amazing would come from the diagnosis, I would have bet them every penny I had against it. It wasn't that I thought the disease would get the best of Joseph—I knew he was stronger than the disease—I just couldn't imagine it would be another step toward success. God's strange gift wrapping struck again though because there we were, watching our healthy son not only live, but conquer the world.

There was an ominous cloud that settled over the brightness of our son's continued success. I mentioned that fearing the loss of my wife was something I never wanted to do again. Well, unfortunately, I didn't really get to call the shots and just four months after the colostomy reversal I had to face my biggest fears all over again and they were much uglier the next time.

During the original surgery that Jo had to reverse the colostomy, her intestines slipped into her pelvis area and the doctors couldn't get them out to attach them together, which they needed to do to eliminate the bag. Fortunately there was a new practice that had come about in which doctors used a kind of surgical staple gun and they were able to staple the intestine to the pelvis and remove the bag. All seemed well at that point. The bag was removed and that intestines back in place.

Josephine returned home after a week in the hospital and her abdomen felt fine considering, but she started complaining that her neck hurt. She brushed it off at first, assuming that when they transferred from bed to bed that whoever was doing the transferring must have done something to hurt her neck in the process. I was a little irritated by the thought of someone being so careless with my wife, but Jo wasn't too upset by it, so I let it slide.

After a few days at home, the pain still didn't subside. Josephine started to get a little concerned by it, so she called our family doctor, who told her to call a brain surgeon. I immediately did not like the suggestion of a brain surgeon. I didn't want to consider why we may need a brain surgeon, but I was going to have to whether I wanted to or not.

We contacted Dr. Sanfillippo in Las Cruces and I took Jo in to get an MRI. We were supposed to be in the clear now. I had already gone through the fearful waiting. I wasn't ready for MRI's; I really wasn't ready for what the doctor had to tell us. The doctors noticed a large growth the size of an orange at the back left hand side of the brain. I couldn't wrap my mind around the words that were ricocheting around between my ears.

"There is no easy way to say this, but none of the options are very hopeful," the doctor explained as I sat wringing my hands.

"What are they?" I didn't really want to know, but I knew that's what you were supposed to ask next.

"You could die on the table, become paralyzed, or have a stroke," the doctor said to my wife as she sat stoically, listening to the possibilities. "It would be best to get your life in order by preparing a will and saying goodbye to your three children and anyone else that you want to say goodbye to."

"Could I please have just this weekend to spend with my children?" was my wife's immediate response.

"I'm sorry, but no. You need to be here no later than tomorrow morning" the doctor said, taking away the last chance we may have to spend time as a family.

I was shattered, absolutely shattered. Nothing short of losing one of my children could have ripped into the core of my being the way those words did. I had to be strong, though. Jo needed me. She had always been strong for me and it was my turn. We turned in all the paperwork to the doctors and then headed home to do one of the hardest things I've ever had to do: tell our kids that mom may not be with us much longer. This was undoubtedly the worst day of my life.

We got home and explained what was going on as best we could. Joseph got up and left the room immediately. I could see the fear and hurt on his face and it was almost too much to bear. I could hear him as he cried in his room. I felt like doing the same. Neither of us could bear thinking about life without Jo; she was not just a mom and a wife, she was our best friend.

The whole thing seemed like such a slap in the face. After all we've been through, why was this happening now? We had already had to deal with a close call and I was sure I didn't have it in me to do it again. Even worse, what if this one wasn't a close call? Life without Jo wasn't really life as far as I was concerned. She was my other half. I didn't know how to live without her; no one did.

I wasn't going to let my wife and best friend go without a fight, so after I heard the news I called Dr. Anthony Lobianco in Philadelphia, a dear family friend and doctor, to tell him what was going on with Josephine and ask if he could find out anything about Dr. Sanfillipo and what kind of neurosurgeon he was.

Dr. Lobianco called back in no time and said we were in amazing hands; Dr. Sanfillipo was an incredible doctor. This news should have settled my mind a bit, but it didn't at all. Regardless of how good he was, my wife was going to have surgery done on her brain in less than twenty-four hours and no amount of reassurance about the capabilities of a doctor would change that. Don't get me wrong, I was glad to hear the news, but I was still terrified. The conversation Josephine had with me later that night escalated my fears.

"I need to talk to dad a minute, guys. Could everyone leave the room and give us some time alone?" my wife said to the kids and her mother after we had dropped the biggest bomb on them they'd ever known.

The kids and Jo's mom left the room and she turned to me. I had never felt so nervous to be in a room with my own wife, but suddenly I felt like I was about to crawl out of my skin. I wanted to burst into tears, to get angry, and to hold her in my arms all at once, but instead I sat and listened.

"Larry, there is a ninety percent chance I won't make it through this surgery." I winced at that, but remained quiet while Josephine continued. "Please take care of our children; let them know that I love them and that I'm very sorry for not being there for them to see them marry or to see all of my grandchildren grow up. You don't worry about me, I'll be fine, but I at least want you to have this message in case I don't make it."

Josephine was worried not about herself, but about our children from the second she heard the diagnosis. She didn't take a second to be scared or to feel sorry for herself; she only thought of the kids.

At 7 a.m. the next morning, Josephine was at the hospital ready to go, or as ready as she could be. They started treatment by administering steroids to help shrink the tumor. After two days of steroids, on a Monday morning my wife—the mother of my children and love of my life—went under the knife.

Twelve hours later, twelve hours that seemed like an eternity, out came my Josephine being rolled to recovery. As she passed, she lifted her head and waved to all of us smiling. Shortly thereafter she fell asleep and slept for four hours straight.

Dr. Sanfillipo called my wife his miracle girl. He told us that we did have to worry about blood clots, stroke, swelling, and infection, so the next thirty days were really high risk, but everything went perfectly. I barely escaped life without my other half once again. We all prayed and thanked God for letting my wife survive.

As we drove away from the hospital when Jo was released, it felt a lot like the day we drove away from the hospital in New Jersey after my printing press accident. I felt, just like I did that day, that I had been given a second shot at life because Josephine Marie was my life. The feeling was a little different in that I actually felt even more blessed knowing that my wife's life was safe than I did years ago when I realized my own life was finally out of jeopardy. I can't say that I would relive the experience if given the chance but I will say I appreciate the perspective that it gave me. The entire episode made me realize how easy it is to take the small things for granted. I was glad that God was giving me the opportunity to cherish every second with my family from that point on.

CHAPTER FIFTEEN

CONQUERING THE WORLD

———⟨∂/∂⟩———

During Josephine's scares, Joseph had left school to be with his mother as much as he could. I admired that about my son as much as I did his drive to succeed; he knew how to prioritize what was important. While Joseph was on his small break making sure Jo was going to be okay, he also made sure that our family company was moving forward, and that it certainly did.

In 1992 the year after my Josephine survived not one surgery that could have taken her life, but two, Joseph's Lite Cookies made its way into 600 stores and also hit the one million dollar mark in sales. Joseph may have been taking a short break from school, but he was definitely not spending his time idle. He was still out on the road, doing demonstrations and helping the company grow, making sure that 1992 would not be the only year we hit a million dollars in sales.

Joseph returned to NMSU the following year in 1993 and started his juggling act again. He divided his week up to be sure he was dedicating the time he needed to managing the company, attending trade shows, making his classes, doing his homework and studying. I don't know how he did it, but Joseph somehow managed to put his all into the company, his studies, and our family. It was as if he didn't know how to do anything without giving 100 percent to it. He was a feat to behold; he still is.

My son went on to receive his Managerial Leadership Degree and Marketing Degree from NMSU in 1997. Within the four years that he was in college, our company hit one great height after the next. While Joseph was plugging away at all his classes and participating in thirteen different organizations (some of which he was the president), he was also helping take our once small company to levels we never imagined. He picked up Kmart stores in both New Mexico and Texas, got the cookies into Wal-Mart stores in Las Cruces, and even received phone calls from Southland Foods to launch our cookies. In the midst of all our growth, we bought another 4,800 square foot plant. The days of cranking out cookies in a 700 square foot makeshift factory on Gold Street were behind us now and we were making our entrance into the big leagues.

The same year that Joseph walked across the stage and received his bachelor's degree, he got an internship with President Reagan in Century City, California (it was the same weekend, actually). How it happened was a little crazy, but with our family's past, nothing was out of the ordinary anymore. It all started with Jo and me getting Joseph what we thought were just birthday gifts from the Ronald Reagan gift shop, but it ended up providing more than just memorabilia for Joseph to keep in his room.

So, it was Joseph's twenty-sixth birthday and we had ordered him a few things from the Ronald Reagan Library and gift shop. When the package arrived, we noticed that they had sent an item that we hadn't ordered, so Joseph called Carolyn Mente, the woman who was in charge of the gift shop, and explained that he had received something that we didn't pay for. I'm sure Miss Mente was a little taken aback by someone calling to say they were undercharged, but our youngest son has always made it a point to do what was right, even if it seemed like a small thing to most people. His unrelenting conscience came in quite handy that day, though. After discussing the unordered item, Joseph and the gift shop supervisor spoke for hours.

"Does President Reagan ever come into the gift shop?" Joseph asked Miss Mente.

"As a matter of fact, he does," she replied. "He actually has an office in Century City, California."

"Really?" Joseph asked, blown away by the thought of President Reagan walking around a gift shop in California.

"Yes, and he may be hiring," Carolyn went on to tell my son. "Let me get you the phone number to call."

Joseph had really thrown himself into politics over the course of his college career. After being asked to run for president of the College Republicans and being taken under the wing by a woman named Dorothy Thomas, a local politician, he had become involved in politics wherever he could and was interested in doing even more, so at the mention of President Reagan hiring, Joseph was beyond himself.

This wasn't just a chance for Joseph to enter into the world of politics in a big way; it was a chance to meet President Reagan whom Joseph had admired since he was just a nine year old boy (yes, where other boys looked up to Superman and Captain America, Joseph thought President Reagan was a real life super hero and talked about him long before he was a registered voter). Joseph was dead set on getting whatever job he could to work for President Reagan.

Like the go-getter that he was, Joseph immediately called the number the woman had given him and found out that there was one opening for a summer internship. Joseph applied and was relentless in his pursuit. He called those people daily to check on the status of his application or to update his résumé. This was the end of his senior year of college when he should've been looking forward to a graduation party and a summer of freedom, but my Joseph only had eyes for that internship and he knew there was a slew of applicants and only one position, so he made it his mission to stand out, and stand out he did. The kid knew how to get what he wanted.

Sure enough, Joseph got the internship. He got the call on a Friday (the day before his graduation ceremony) to report to California on the following Monday, so he walked across the graduation stage with the class of 1997 (with a 4.0 GPA and belonging to thirteen organizations), then packed up his little Honda Accord, and left for Los Angeles.

Joseph made it out to California in one piece and there he worked at the office with President Reagan and at the foundation with Carolyn Mente and the foundation chairman doing book signings with First Lady Nancy Reagan. Joseph had to take a small break from the business at that time, but the experience he gained was well worth the time he had to spend away. I was worried a little about Joseph being all the way in California. I took solace in the fact that that Paul Smith and the Anthony and Phyllis DeFranco (family friends of ours) were there to watch after him (he ended up going to their homes for dinner on the weekends), but it was still quite a distance and he was still our youngest son. After his first phone call, however, I knew Joseph would be just fine.

"Hello," I said as I picked up the phone in the kitchen.

"Dad? Get mom on the phone. Quick," Joseph panted into the phone.

"Everything okay out there, Joseph?" I asked a little concerned with the urgency in his hurried, breathy words.

"Yeah, yeah. It's great, dad. That's why I want Mom to hear. Is she there?" Joseph went on.

"Jo! Pick up the phone. It's Joseph," I yelled into the living room.

"Hi, hon. How's the job?" Jo asked Joseph as she picked up the living room phone.

"You are never going to believe what happened to me today," Joseph blurted.

"Well, tell us," Jo replied.

"I met President Reagan, mom and dad! I met him in person. He came straight up to me," Joseph was almost yelling at that point he was so excited.

"Oh my gosh, Joseph. That is amazing. What'd you say to him?" I asked.

"All I could say was 'It's an honor to meet you, Mr. President.' All these years and I was so nervous that's all I could say," Joseph was still rushing through his words trying to get them out before the shock wore off.

"I couldn't have said it better myself, son," I told him.

"I am so proud of you, Joseph," Jo chimed in.

"Look at what your hard work has done."

"I just can't believe it. I can't believe I met him," Joseph went on, hardly noticing our responses he was so wrapped up in the moment. "He even called himself 'Ronnie' when he introduced himself. Can you believe that?"

"Well, I certainly can," I said to Joseph. "You already told us almost two decades ago you would meet President Reagan some day, so I can believe it."

I looked at Josephine as Joseph went on to tell us all about his first meeting with President Reagan and we both smiled. Joseph just kept repeating how unbelievable the whole thing was, but we knew our son would meet President Reagan some day. He had set his mind when he was nine that he would, so we knew it was only a matter of time. With Joseph, everything was just a matter of time once he put his mind to it.

Joseph not only got to meet President Reagan, but he also came back with quite a story about him that we love to share over dinner and will always be able to tell our grandkids and their kids. On one occasion, President Reagan went to Joseph's desk to see how he was doing. While he was asking, he snuck into the small kitchen that was right in front of Joseph's desk, reached one hand after another into a jar full of jelly beans, and grabbed two handfuls. He emptied one into his pocket and kept the others in his hand. As President Reagan stood popping the jelly beans in his mouth, Joseph got a phone call from the chief of staff asking if the president was with him. Joseph confirmed that President Reagan was in fact there, and then the chief of staff said she was on her way and to keep the president out of the jelly beans. Upon arriving, the chief of staff she asked President Reagan if he was eating jelly beans before lunch. To this he chuckled. When she asked again if he had jelly beans, he replied with a, "No, only a couple," then winked at Joseph with a grin and walked off back to his office.

During his internship Joseph also learned a valuable lesson from the former first lady. While working at a book signing with Mrs. Reagan, Joseph saw something special in that petite woman with a giant personality he knew that he wanted to emulate. During a book signing people brought the books over they wanted signed and Joseph would hand them to the first lady. The signing was to last four hours, but Mrs. Reagan sat there and signed books until every single person got a signed copy, which ended up taking over nine hours. Joseph never took a break, never went to the restroom, and never stopped to eat anything the entire day.

At the end of the book signing, Joseph and the first lady went upstairs so Mrs. Reagan could finally eat her lunch. She grabbed half of her tuna fish sandwich and tried to hand it to Joseph to eat.

"No thank you, Mrs. Reagan. I'm fine," my son said to the first lady as she handed over half her sandwich.

"I noticed you never took a break. Are you going to tell the first lady no?" Mrs. Reagan said.

"I guess not," Joseph said and then the two of them shared a tuna fish sandwich.

Joseph admired Mrs. Reagan more than ever that day. He saw that she was not only driven, but that she was sweet and compassionate, too, and she always kept others in mind. That internship was definitely a highlight for Joseph and our family.

After Joseph returned from his internship, it was back to business and business was booming, and changing. We discontinued fructose cookies and launched Sugar Free Joseph's Cookies which were crispy instead of soft and made it to the 2,000 mark with the number of distributors who were selling our product. Every time that I thought we couldn't possibly grow any larger, we did. Although we took a small chance changing the cookies' consistency, it ended up proving to be a good move on our part and, two years after we changed the formula, those new crispy cookies ended up landing us a deal with Bloomingdales. I'll tell you, seeing our family's cookies in a store like Bloomingdales was a true triumph. Being in grocery stores and health food stores was an accomplishment, but making it to Bloomingdales was a dream—a dream come true in our case.

The same year we had reached the shelves of Bloomingdales, we had to make a drastic change in how we did business. The adjustments we had to make served as a little speed bump for our business, but my son Joseph had become quite the business-minded young man and was able to get us through the modified processes without too much trouble.

The problem we faced in 1999 was that we were having trouble with labor and finding good, reliable people to work for our ever expanding company. Knowing that NAFTA was going to create more international competition, Joseph and I both knew that the only way to survive long term was to reduce regulation and labor costs, but my son and I agreed that we would not let go of any of our team members to do so. They had families just like we did and their livelihood was important. I knew firsthand what could happen when you're left jobless and I wasn't about to let any of my people experience that and neither was Joseph.

So, we had to think of some way to save our company without putting any of our team members out of work. Luckily for us, Joseph knew just what to do; he put in place a hiring freeze, which meant he could avoid firing any team members. We needed to keep costs down without letting people go, and the hiring freeze ensured that payroll didn't rise, but at the same time no one currently employed would be sent to the unemployment lines. He also invested in packaging equipment that would eliminate most of so many workers' handling of the cookies. Our original process required several hands to do several different jobs. The cookies had to be deposited onto pans, cooled in racks for forty-five minutes, and placed into trays. After that someone had to weigh trays, place trays into bags, seal the bags, and date code each bag.

It didn't stop there, either. The bags then went through their own process in which they were placed into boxes that had to be date coded, taped, and placed on pallets. We decided to look into new, revolutionary equipment that would alter the entire process.

With the introduction of the new equipment, which was a brand new kind of equipment and innovative to the business, several of the processes were done by conveyor belts and machinery, which eliminated the amount of hands needed and sped the process up. Our new method was ground-breaking and we were the first to use it and the equipment, so it was a little risky, but paid off big in the end. We knew that we had to reduce labor costs and decrease production costs, and the equipment did just that. We wouldn't be able to employ anybody, after all, if the company didn't survive.

Joseph's decision to do a hiring freeze did just what it needed to do; it ensured the livelihood of the company and allowed for even more growth in the future. We had been threatened by regulations that were beyond our control, but Joseph's ability to solve big problems and maintain the integrity of the company got us through the ordeal and we didn't let down any of our team members. He really never does cease to amaze me. Thanks to his solution, our company went on to accomplish more success. We were included in the Weight Watchers Book and were approved by Kmart for a national launch. The Weight Watchers Book was a success; the Kmart deal, however almost ended up being a disaster.

What happened with Kmart was this: we started to really court Kmart at a national level, but it took several years to close the account. We were anxious to get Kmart because they were going to be a huge account for us. The buyer for the store, Barry Phillips (who was also a visionary who knew the importance of carrying sugar free cookies for their customers) finally made the commitment to carry the cookies and gave an estimated order size of over $1,000,000. This was no small deal.

After giving us an estimate on order size, however, the buyer postponed the order, which was a pretty big disappointment to me and Joseph; it was like trying to reel in a big catch that just won't give in. We knew that million dollar deal was on the line, but it kept fighting us. We tried to stay optimistic, though, and be patient.

Something happened months later that really made our jaws drop. Where we were praying for the store to finalize the deal, our tone suddenly changed and we were thanking God for the buyer's decision to put the order on hold. The reason for the abrupt attitude change was that not too long after we were discouraged by the massive order being placed on hold, Kmart went bankrupt. Talk about a blessing in disguise. The Kmart order never came through, but if it would have then we would have gone bankrupt with them because we would have had shipped a million dollars of product to a company that was no longer paying their bills.

Another stroke of bad luck turned into something good for the Semprevivos. I didn't forget to count that blessing and neither did my son. Because we saw how the bankruptcies of other companies could create financial hardships for our company, we decided to always run our company by controlled growth to ensure that we never overextended or put our company in harm's way.

CHAPTER SIXTEEN

ICING ON THE COOKIE

The same year that a postponed order allowed us to miraculously escape financial ruin, our son's once small cookie company that brought in $20,000 a year (and we thought that was big time then) expanded to a 52,000 square foot factory and it even opened a Florida office for accounting. Joseph had just turned thirty years old the year before and he was running a company that had offices in multiple states. I knew he was destined for great things, but that didn't make any of his accomplishments less amazing and, as a father, I was totally impressed with my son.

I sometimes couldn't believe what a success our company had achieved. Sure, I knew that I had an incredible son with the most impressive work ethic and strongest drive I'd ever witnessed, but still I would marvel at this thriving business that started with just the Semprevivo family in a cramped, little factory. To this day I sit back at times and think, all this from a diabetes diagnosis. That's what it was, after all, that got us into this whole thing; a diagnosis that originally said my son wouldn't make it to see his twenties.

In 2003, just around fourteen years after doctors told us Joseph would be lucky to celebrate his twenty-first birthday, we had to double the office space in Florida for sales and customer service, and the next year in 2004 we had to add 4,000 additional square feet to the factory in New Mexico. Sometimes doctors don't take into account the will of the patient when they're handing out a diagnosis. They had certainly underestimated Joseph back in 1980. That's one of the things I guess that has made all of Joseph' success so remarkable to me; because Joseph's success didn't start with the sugar free ice cream, it started when he was diagnosed with diabetes. Every year that he chose not to give into the original doctor's prognosis of not living to see his twenties, Joseph was triumphant. That he had built a thriving company along the way was just icing on the cake, or the cookie, in our case.

With all the growth and success, Joseph began to receive some pretty impressive awards for the company he had begun to build the day he walked into our family kitchen and scared his mother to death with strawberry ice cream smeared across his face. It's funny that, no matter how old you are or how old your kids may be, a parent feels the same pride in their children's accomplishments—that a thirty-year-old son's business success is just as exciting as an infant's first words or an eight-year-old's first merit badge. Pride in children is timeless and has no age limit. My kids have definitely taught me that.

Each time Joseph got a letter or phone call about a new award, I beamed brighter and brighter with the pride I felt for my son. He received an Alumni Award from his Alma Mater, which I watched him receive with tears in my eyes. After that, the awards only got more remarkable. In 2005 Joseph received the Governor's VIVA (Vision, Investment, Vitality, Action) Award from Governor Richardson. I had received this award myself almost twenty years before, so it was quite a moving moment to see my son receive the award as well. I would say I was passing the torch, but I feel that Joseph and I were both holding it the entire time.

A PBS and CNN appearance later, Joseph went on to receive the most prestigious business award that a chief executive officer can receive. Joseph was named Best Business Executive of 2005 by the Stevie Awards, which are the like the Oscars of the business world. To receive a Stevie Award is like being placed in the executive hall of fame. I watched my son walk up to the stage and do just that. I was so proud of him; I kept telling him it was his moment to shine, but he felt it was our moment. As I sat out in the sea of faces and stared up at my youngest son as he approached the podium, I couldn't imagine being any prouder. As he began to speak, I saw what an amazing guy I had raised. I beamed as Joseph took his place behind the microphone and accepted his award.

"This means so much to me," Joseph started.

"And I want to dedicate this award to my mom and dad, Josephine and Lawrence Semprevivo. Without them, I would be nothing. I would actually like my dad to come up to help me accept the award."

As Joseph said those words, a knot tightened in my throat and I had to fight back tears. I had told him with every award that it was *his* time, but he would always insist that the awards were *ours*, not just his. Joseph wasn't in it for the glory, so he couldn't just accept the award and take credit for all he'd done. He always recognized his family as the root of his success. There was a part of me that wanted my son to own his achievements, but there was also a part of me that was indescribably touched by my son's selflessness.

Joseph's willingness to share the limelight wasn't the only way that he showed me how much he loved and appreciated me. Joseph got me my dream car, a 1957 Chevy convertible, for my seventieth birthday. It wasn't just the car that was so important, but what it meant. Joseph knew that I had given up the same model car decades ago to help make ends meet for the family, so he got me another just like the one I sold so many years ago. He also did something that meant even more to me than giving me a classic car; he introduced me to one star after the next, which has been one of the highlights of my life.

See, I have always been intrigued by show business, and particularly standup comedians. There's something insanely impressive about anyone who can stand up in front of a crowd of people and make everyone in the room laugh. I would've loved to have been able to do it myself, actually. Since it wasn't in the cards for me to be a performer myself, though, I loved meeting them every chance I got. I thought that my brush with Hollywood that was made possible by Paul Smith would be the only time I would get to actually rub elbows with stars. Most people don't get the opportunity to have a conversation with celebrities even once, so I supposed I could be content with that, but Joseph had different ideas.

Joseph decided that he would use the success he had experienced to do something special for me. I loved comedy shows, so one time Joseph surprised Jo and me with tickets to see David Spade. When we got there, we realized we were right in the front. I was blown away. That wasn't it, though. After the show, Joseph took us backstage and I actually got to sit and talk to the one and only David Spade. I couldn't believe that I was actually sitting in the same room and having a conversation with him. I was impressed with the front row seats, and now here I was behind the scenes. I was like a kid in a candy store. I couldn't get enough.

Luckily for me, I have a son who can't give enough, so Joseph began to make it a regular routine to get me in to meet movie stars, famous comedians, and even screenwriters. I got to meet stars like Dick Van Dyke, Burt Reynolds, and Kevin James just to name a few. I even met sports super stars and hall of famers like Muhammad Ali, Joe Frasier, and Dwight Howard. Each time Joseph took us to meet a new person I was awed by the experience. It wasn't that I saw these people as superhuman; if anything I've come to realize that celebrities are just people, too, and that's why the meetings have made such an impact. I would've never thought that a celebrity would take time to chat with me, but I have found that isn't true at all.

Joseph taking me to meet so many seemingly untouchable stars has given me memories and stories that I can hold onto forever. That is what life is about, too; the memories that we make and the good experiences we have to hang on to. More than anything, Joseph taking me to meet so many talented people I admire has proved to me that I have raised a man who is unbelievably thoughtful and has never, ever left anyone in the dust from the trails he has blazed. As a parent, you can achieve no success greater than having your children grow to become great people. I don't mean to brag, but I can easily say my children have done that, and of that I am shamelessly proud.

Joseph has always made it a point to do all he can to keep our relationship a priority in his life. It can be tough sometimes for adults and their parents to remain close with so much going on in life, but the love that Joseph was conceived in seems to never fade with time. My son goes out of his way to be sure that I receive as much love as he feels I have given him. He has, for example, made it a point to see me become an honorary initiate in his college Fraternity, Pi Kappa Alpha. His doing so meant we could have a closer bond now that he is fully grown and has a life of his own outside of Jo, me, and his siblings.

It may seem like a small thing, but you always fear as a parent that your kids will outgrow you. Although I know Joseph is his own man now, that he still includes me in his life so much means the world to me. As I see the love that is always in him for his family and the dedication he has to all of us, I am reminded of the words of the Monsignor the day of my accident, of the immense feeling of love I had in the wake of the tragedy, and of the way I knew that Jo and I were supposed to have another child. Looking at my son, I realize that he is why I had that urge to have another—that he is the manifestation of the love that I felt.

My pride in my son has grown even more since he has had children of his own. Joseph is now the father of three amazing little boys and a beautiful little girl who have a way of melting my heart with a simple little giggle.

Unfortunately, Joseph's eldest was diagnosed with diabetes at only ten months old. He is five now, but I remember the diagnosis like it happened last week. It was a very familiar scene.

When Joseph and his wife had their first son, our entire family was elated. Everyone loves a new baby in the family. Of course, because Joseph's diabetes, we were also a little worried that little Joseph would come to be diabetic as well. Because of this, Joseph and his wife started doing blood sugar tests immediately and regularly to be sure they didn't miss it. Joseph turned out to be as diligent and thoughtful a father as he is a businessman.

At ten months old, just days after a doctor's visit, Joseph was cuddling little Joseph and he noticed something was off.

"Little Joseph is diabetic," Joseph said to his wife, Memory.

"That's impossible, Joseph. We just took him to the doctor and we've been testing his blood sugar," Memory replied.

Joseph went on to explain the symptoms he had seen in their son. Memory thought that Joseph may have been overreacting a bit, but she wasn't going to take chances and Joseph was serious about this, so they took little Joseph to the hospital.

They found that Little Joseph was, in fact, diabetic. It had just happened, though. Joseph was so in tune with his son, he noticed the very day that it happened. Upon hearing the diagnosis, we were all naturally a little fearful because little Joseph was so young and unable to tell anyone how he felt, which could have been a real obstacle. Joseph and Memory decided to be proactive instead of afraid, though, and they found their way around Little Joseph's inability to talk. They put their all into making sure little Joseph was safe and healthy.

To this day, Joseph and Memory do constant tests to make sure that little Joseph's levels are good. Even if it's three in the morning and his blood sugar is high, little Joseph is taken out of bed to exercise. We had a conversation about Joseph's sacrifice and dedication to little Joseph once.

"I'm really proud of how you're handling this, Joseph," I said to my son one day.

"What do you mean?" Joseph asked.

"I mean how dedicated you are to little Joseph to make sure he's healthy. It isn't easy never sleeping through the night to do constant blood test. I'm just proud of you and Memory and how selfless you've been," I explained.

"It should look familiar, dad," Joseph said.

"What should?" I wasn't sure what he meant.

"The sleepless nights and the midnight jogs.

You did the same thing for me when I was a kid, dad. I'm just doing what I was taught to do by you and mom for our son," Joseph said.

He was right, I realized. We had done the same exact thing when he was a kid. I never thought of it as a sacrifice. It was just what we did and, as long as it meant Joseph was going to be okay, it didn't matter if I never slept a full night again. He is now doing the same for his son. The cycle of diabetes is very unfortunate. The cycle of loving fathers, however, is quite amazing and I'm glad I can say I have been a part of it.

Little Joseph's diagnosis, like so many other obstacles our family has faced, has made our family stronger and it has also showed me that I can exhale, relax a little, and pat myself on the back for having done all I ever wanted to do as a father. I have taught my children what it is to be a good parent and I have also instilled a love in them that trickles down onto others. Yes, my family has built a successful business that has opened doors in the world of diabetic eating, but most importantly my family has built an unbreakable bond that rests on the foundation of overcoming the odds by fighting harder, staying positive, and sticking together. Not one of us would be where we are today if not for dedication to one another and perseverance.

What I would like to leave you with and what I believe that Joseph's Lite Cookies is symbolic for is this: life is full of good and bad no matter who you are; because of this, it isn't our circumstances or what happens to us by chance that will make or break us, it is what we do in response to the situations that arise in life. My accident, a bankrupt business, Joseph's diabetes, my wife's back-to-back near fatal health conditions; all of these things I and my family could have faltered to, but we didn't. We started where we could, worked together, and battled our way out of everything.

What I have learned from life is this: when I refused to succumb to my fate, my fate would succumb to my will—and from every near tragedy a triumph emerged.

EPILOGUE
by Joseph Semprevivo

The day I handed my dad a report card with a C on it was the day that I realized my own life philosophy and I have lived by it ever since. That philosophy is simple; only 100 percent is good enough and if you aren't willing to put your all into something, you may as well not even attempt it. One important lesson I have learned through my trials and tribulations is success doesn't come easy; it's always fluid, always moving with peaks and valleys. Because success can be slippery, the only way to achieve it and maintain it is to give everything you've got every moment you can. Because of this, I break my weeks down not only by days, but by hours, and I take full advantage of every hour I have by filling each with meaningful activities. My time goes only to that which matters and nothing else, which is my work and my family because it is in these two things only that true success is found.

I have built my own success on hard work and the support of my family. You don't have to be born wealthy, have the right name, or have opportunities handed to you to become a true success. All you need is hard work, dedication, and a support system that stands behind you no matter what. I know this because I have seen it firsthand watching my parents and have experienced it in my own life building my own company from the ground up. Neither my dad nor I have been given anything; we haven't inherited wealth or fallen into success overnight. We haven't even had an easy road where luck is concerned, but we did it all together and we never gave up on one another.

None of the trials my family faced stopped us because we knew that if we worked hard enough, our time would come and it certainly has. Joseph's Lite Cookies is now a debt-free company and I have been invited and appeared on CNBC not once, but twice, (I appeared on both "How I Made My Millions" and "The Big Idea") to explain how I've achieved my success and to tell my story, and my story is this: I am just a guy from Deming, New Mexico who was raised by struggling middle-class parents whose love and dedication to their family pulled them through every hardship and taught them how to live a life of no regrets. I wasn't a Rockefeller or the heir to a hotel fortune; I was a young Italian kid in a dusty New Mexico town who knew I wanted to make a difference somehow and I had parents who, through their love and guidance, gave me the tools to do that.

So many people I have met tell me how things *can't* be done, how hard things are, or how they just want to take the easy road. These kind of people have never truly been pushed or witnessed what struggling families have witnessed; instead they feel entitled, privileged, and want success handed to them. Dreams don't often just come true, though; they are made. Dreams are the product of hard work, sacrifice, and commitment; they are not fairy tales that just come to people. There is no wishing well that will bring you your life's aspirations and no serendipitous moment around the bend that will lead you to success. *You* make your dreams come true, *you* make your life everything you want it to be, and *you* do all you can to create moments that will lead you to success and you must take advantage of the opportunities that come your way.

Finally, people often like to blame circumstance on their failures in life; they want to say that the successful ones are those who had everything going for them from the get-go. I am proof that is not true. My family has overcome one obstacle after the next to create success. We have learned that we are in control of our fate and that nothing can steal our dreams as long as we always try harder. You have the choice when things go wrong to be the victor or the victim; always be the victor. After all, success always tastes so much sweeter after the bitterness of impending defeat. You will never make it past the bitter if you let the setbacks stop you, so keep going and always know that the difference between failure and success isn't money, background, what you were born with, or even the hand that life has dealt you ; it is *you*. What you do and how you chose to respond to adversity is what separates the happily-ever-after's from the maybe-next-time's or the never-will's. When tragedy stands in your way, make something good of it and turn it into a triumph.

 e|LIVE

listen|imagine|view|experience

AUDIO BOOK DOWNLOAD INCLUDED WITH THIS BOOK!

In your hands you hold a complete digital entertainment package. In addition to the paper version, you receive a free download of the audio version of this book. Simply use the code listed below when visiting our website. Once downloaded to your computer, you can listen to the book through your computer's speakers, burn it to an audio CD or save the file to your portable music device (such as Apple's popular iPod) and listen on the go!

How to get your free audio book digital download:

1. Visit www.tatepublishing.com and click on the e|LIVE logo on the home page.
2. Enter the following coupon code:
   3f20-ac49-279b-1257-24d2-12b1-9d82-b6f7
3. Download the audio book from your e|LIVE digital locker and begin enjoying your new digital entertainment package today!

9 781622 958818